Habits Switcher

A Fundamental Treatment of How to Develop Good Habits to Change Your Life. The Essential Guide to reset Your Mind and Build The Better You

By

Christabel Ziegler

© Copyright 2020 by (Christabel Ziegler) - All rights reserved.

This document is geared towards providing exact and reliable information in regards to the topic and issue covered. The publication is sold with the idea that the publisher is not required to render accounting, officially permitted, or otherwise, qualified services. If advice is necessary, legal or professional, a practiced individual in the profession should be ordered.

- From a Declaration of Principles which was accepted and approved equally by a Committee of the American Bar Association and a Committee of Publishers and Associations.

In no way is it legal to reproduce, duplicate, or transmit any part of this document in either electronic means or in printed format. Recording of this publication is strictly prohibited and any storage of this document is not allowed unless with written permission from the publisher. All rights reserved.

The information provided herein is stated to be truthful and consistent, in that any liability, in terms of inattention or otherwise, by any usage or abuse of any policies, processes, or directions contained within is the solitary and utter responsibility of the recipient reader. Under no circumstances will any legal responsibility or blame be held against the publisher for any reparation, damages, or monetary loss due to the information herein, either directly or indirectly.

Respective authors own all copyrights not held by the publisher.

The information herein is offered for informational purposes solely, and is universal as so. The presentation of the information is without contract or any type of guarantee assurance.

The trademarks that are used are without any consent, and the publication of the trademark is without permission or backing by the trademark owner. All trademarks and brands within this book are for clarifying purposes only and are the owned by the owners themselves, not affiliated with this document.

Table of Content

INTRODUCTION 6

CHAPTER 1: DEFINITION OF HABITS SWITCHER 8

1.1 Habit Switcher a Discipline 8

1.2 Start day with Meditation 11

1.3 Altering Habits Switcher 11

1.4 Point to Ponder Altering Habits Switcher 16

CHAPTER 2: HABITS SWITCHER FOR BETTER MIND AND PHYSICAL FITNESS 24

2.1 Physical Activity 24

2.2 Habits Switcher for Good Job and Performance 26

2.3 Little Better Relationship Habits 28

2.4 Plan Your Day Throughout the Year 30

CHAPTER 3: HABITS SWITCHER FOR PROFESSIONALS 36

3.1 Be Open. 36

3.2 Keep Communicating 37

3.3 Complete Your Hardest Task First 42

3.4 Break Down Your Big Goals into Smaller Goals 44

CHAPTER 4: BE LESS REACTIVE AND MORE PROACTIVE 50

4.1 Tips to React Less 50

4.2 Don't React What You See on Social Media 52

4.3 Manage Your Attention, Not Your Time 54

CHAPTER 5: HABITS SWITCHER FOR BUSINESSMEN..59

5.1 Find a Mentor... 59

5.2 Reach Former Colleagues 61

5.3 Build a Customer Centric Culture in Your Organization 64

5.4 Humbleness 69

5.5 Ask for help from Experts... 71

CHAPTER 6: HABITS SWITCHER FOR KIDS 74

6.1 Opting Physical Activities & Healthy Diet............................. 74

6.2 Be Courteous & Unbiased 78

6.3 Stay Clean & Hygienic 80

6.4 Having A Healthy and Positive Mind-Set.............................. 82

CHAPTER 7: PESSIMIST MINDSET- HURDLE IN ALTERING HABITS SWITCHER 86

7.1 Pessimist Mindset 86

7.2 Anxiety and Frustration 92

7.3 Identifying Core Objective 99

7.4 Explore your Favorite Things to Do..................................... 100

CONCLUSION 104

REFERENCE 106

Introduction

Habits Switcher in our life may have various categories, or they will be different in professionals, businessmen or among kids. Habits Switcher can be classified in as – be a good listener, finding a mentor, cultivating the relationships, keeping nerves in control, having a strong willpower, self-control not emotionally driven, and staying clean and hygienic etc. It helps us stay career focused, help us to deal adaptively with distractions, be a disciplined citizen and it will ultimately help us to accomplish what we have planned in our life.

If you are interested in learning more about How Habits Switcher in Life can lead to dramatic change in your life and how you can alter your pessimist mind and adapt positive approach, this book has everything you are looking for. It will give you tips ranging from what internal and external factors can have an impact on your pessimist mindset, how you can cope up with them and what are the best Habits Switcher which can change your life. I have classified Habits Switcher among professionals, businessmen and kids. Each habit will seem like a small one but in sum it can have a great impact in your life and personality. Experts have linked having a Few-habits with accomplishment, others with well-being, and still others argue that it's has a direct influence on the personality.

Some professionals make life seem easy and straight forward by opting Habits Switcher in daily routine even it seems like a small one. We quickly get through the hardest days without blinking an eye, and even in the toughest of conditions appear to feel upbeat just because of the positive mindset. These people are much the same as you. In reality they share similar anxieties and emotions but have a strong control over it. Nevertheless, what separates the productive and the unsuccessful is not genetic material or ability, yet its habits, its priorities and, in particular, its positive habits.

Habits Switcher are the qualities that still lack in our daily life despite of whatever profession you have. If you have trouble figuring out how to enrich your personality with Few good habits, how to keep your mind away from pessimist approach or unhealthy habits, how to indulge your personality in positive habits through various exercises, tactics, what are the benefits of Habits Switcher and what is the skillset of a person who is adaptive to Habits Switcher? This book has covered all the untapped area of above-mentioned questions and much more.

It also covers that how transforming pessimist mindset into optimistic mindset, how unhealthy activities/habits of professionals, youngsters and kids are different. We need to change the surrounding in order to opt good Habits Switcher so positive energy can be gained which will lead for a disciplined life. All these exercise, tips and researches will help you to opt the "Habits Switcher" in your life and ultimately it will help you start a journey toward bright future.

Chapter 1: Definition of Habits Switcher

Whether you're on a diet or exercising, learning, doing company, or preparing for anything you want to do, good habits is needed to achieve your objectives, live a healthy lifestyle, and, last but not least, be comfortable. People with high levels of good Habits Switcher don't encourage impulsive impulses and emotions to influence their decisions. Disciplined people always make rational choices with the future outcome in mind, so they don't get too stressed and upset if their choices collapse.

Habits Switcher can be educated and improved, just like any other talent. The post should instruct you on how good habits will change. That is an important skill you need to have if you want to be effective. Whether in school or at work, good habits are essential in all aspects of life. In this essay, we will discuss the Importance of well disciplining oneself. Although most people today know its value for our everyday lives, it is actively practiced by only a few individuals. People say having good habits implies being harsh on yourself, depriving you of being joyful, being a type of person like "Destroy Joy," but that's not real. Getting good habits is having control of the behaviour, feelings, choices, even the (well sometimes) animalistic reactions of our individual.

1.1 Habit Switcher a Discipline

Habits Switcher is a highly desirable attribute for many people; still, an elusive attribute that slips through our fingers too often. Throughout everyday life, there are a host of places where so many of us want to do better. This is especially evident given the millions who make New Year's resolutions every year.

These strategies also include targets related to diet and exercise, health, relationships, and smoking reduction. Unfortunately, however, for such attempts, an 80 percent failure rate has been reported. However, general efforts to change Habits Switcher result in a relapse about half of the time. Why are we so disappointed by our insufficient efforts to improve ourselves? Such targets, for one thing, are not easy. The happiness of one's dreams "takes a tremendous amount of determination, dedication, good habit, and effort" This book on "how to change Habits Switcher" will examine the research behind self-control and good habit (terms to be used interchangeably), including its many benefits and how to attain them. There will also be several interesting research studies outlined.

When you wonder why discipline is necessary, discipline will make you more successful if you are someone with goals in life. People who are highly organized do not tolerate procrastination to come into their lives. I realize this is going to be a bit complicated for a freshly educated person who wants to get better in life. But as you keep practicing eliminating all the obstacles from your ambitions, studying now, and then how to meditate, you will be more successful than ever. Many citizens who are controlled do not have unproductive behaviors such as playing games (unless you are a professional gamer). Disciplined people can play games, so they make sure it's planned and on their list of activities. Do not do anything because of impulsive impulses or emotions; instead, make decisions based on more important goals.

Individuals who are controlled also find ways to ease their jobs. They plan their activities for optimum efficiency. They treat their time well in order to achieve their full potential as a person. You even learn how to delegate tasks to the right people so they can accomplish things even quicker with their experience.

This is as simple as this: They are happy with getting the things they desire. Add it in your file if you wish to help others! Would you like to be an engineer, an artist, a scientist, a model, and a doctor? Make a plan, and don't feel nervous about how you're going to do it. Head right ahead and work your way to achieving everything you desired! Simple washing dishes will make you feel good, or maybe taking a bath, or perhaps having a shower for your dog, or cleaning your feet, or maybe learning a topic in school, or getting high scores. The more things you do, the happier it will make you feel. One of the benefits of lifetime training is that it offers us more focus. Achieving goals in line often take time and effort. Disciplined candidates are likely to pass an exam along with those who are not. Disciplined competitors are more likely to win a competition than those not. Discipline will carry you anywhere you wish. It allows you a more sense of direction towards the future in which procrastination and entertaining threats cannot offer you.

People who practice balancing their time and work are developing greater awareness. To them, it is second nature to consider different possible obstacles that will prevent them from achieving their goals. High knowledge can allow you to notice things that may enable you to accomplish tasks faster. In a corporate environment, a higher level of understanding is built as you go more senior positions within the organizational structure. These days not so many individuals are highly disciplined. If you have one, you will be stared at by others as if you are some sort of a superhero character who can perform several things in a short amount of time. Another thing to note here is that responsible people know how to take accountability and take responsibility.

This is where you get the most love for yourself. Only a few people take the confidence to be scolded if something went wrong.

During these cases, people with high self-control excel as they know how to handle things properly, including the emotions involved. You want to maintain a good health condition, as you become more successful. You don't want to skip out on the chance to do more simply by having the common flu or any other kind of disease. Monitor the urge to eat junk foods and supplement them all with balanced products.

1.2 Start day with Meditation

Meditation is another subject to be included. Physical health is one of those issues that we need to think for, but also mental health. Through practicing meditation daily, we will be able to declutter our minds with all kinds of mental garbage, which drains and distracts us from getting our work done quickly. Meditation often helps to control our inner being by getting a more optimistic outlook in life, as we can simply chuck out all the bad things that appear in our heads. A key to success is to be optimistic about everything. Overall, the controlled are satisfied than the non-disciplined. They are finding ways and making decisions to avoid possible issues that may arise throughout their lives. Good habits may also boost one's attitude, as they learn how to cope and deal with different types of situations in times of trouble. Attaining targets is a measure of success that offers gratification that undoubtedly contributes to happiness for an individual.

1.3 Altering Habits Switcher

How to keep Habits Switcher If you could just pick one or two (or seven) habits to create in the next few months-habits that will have the most impact on your life, what would they be? This question I often get asked because people are overwhelmed when it comes to starting positive changes in life.

They're asking me: What should one or two habits start with? It is not an easy matter. I've undergone so many changes, from quitting smoking to simplifying my life to reducing debt to many more. And they all seemed to be life-changing, and they all seemed significant. But if I began again, and had to choose one or two, it would be the one or two below mentioned. The following list is in order of what I think I would do the first 6-7 months of changing my life. But understand that each person is different. Nobody should exactly follow my choices— you have to figure out what works for you.

At the same time, take on two or more patterns. We've done all of that. I want to learn to wake early, to start running, to eat healthily, to be more disciplined, and to compose. All at once, every day! But no matter how enthusiastic we are about all these goals, even taking on just two/three habits at a time is setting ourselves up for failure. I just tried it. Multiple times. It is certainly possible, but it is not for those of us who are having trouble changing habits (I think that's almost all of us). I would estimate that if you focus on one habit at a time, one month at a time, you'll triple or even quadruple your chances of success. Devote all your attention to breaking the habit, and then move on to the next one once it's on autopilot. Knock'em down one after the other.

Not committing paper strategy. Waking up quickly, leaping out of bed and screaming out loud, "I'm going to make a change today! "Who amongst us did not do this? (Side note: if you don't live alone, your friends or family members may not appreciate all the yelling.) But it's not enough just to reassure ourselves, loudly or softly in our heads, that we'll improve. You have to get your goal written down. Write down the start date.

The end date published (30 days is a good time frame). Just write down what you are going to do.

Write down how you'll be responsible, what are your incentives, what are the challenges, what are your causes. Below for more on these. The main thing: put it on paper and stick to the plan (don't put the plan in your inbox, you'll piler it!).

I've practiced this for myself a couple of times: I'm going to say, "I think I'm going to quit smoking today." Then I'm going to throw away my pack of cigarettes (this should be in the past as I'm not smoking anymore, but I'm too lazy to go back and change the tension). Then I'll go (often half a day!) for as long as I can, and then cave in and go buy another pack. Then I feel guilty for a while until I commit half to quit again. That is not working. You have Big Time to commit. Which means telling the world. Honestly — put it on your blog, tell your family, friends, bosses, your butcher, the high school guy you're saying hello to when you run into him at the grocery store and call him "buddy," because you've forgotten his name. The more humans, the stronger. Upload your complete plan. Put a sign onto your desk and fridge. Make a solemn promise to your child (when quitting smoking, that worked for me). There'll be moments when, almost inevitably, you falter. When you need support, to whom do you turn? If you don't have a good answer to this, then you have to think through it. That is a good choice if you have a significant other, but have more than one supporter. Perhaps your mother, your dad, your best friend, your boss. Maybe a friend online, or three. Better still, enter a support group or an online forum full of like-minded people. Make them commit and ask them to help you when you hit rough spots. If you do, make a promise to call them. Bring that into your proposal in writing.

Through my experience, I call motivation what people call discipline. Why do you get enough discipline to do something? Because the right inspiration is in you. You lose discipline when you lose motivation.

Think through your reasons before you launch your change of habit. Why are you doing just that? When you forget your reasons, what will keep you going? Of course, public engagement is a great motivator, but you should also have internal ones. Write down those in your plan. Any change of habit is a road riddled with obstacles. Unfortunately, we often quit when we hit some of these. Or we're going to try again, but with the same result, we hit the same obstacles again and again. Alternatively, think through it, and predict the obstacles. Thought about what challenge stopped you if you struggled before. If you've never changed the habit before, do some research and read about others that have achieved and failed to do so, to find out what challenges you can face. Then make a plan of what you're going to do when facing the obstacles. For example, when I go out, I have difficulty eating in moderation. What am I going to do when I come out to eat? What is my strategy? I've got to think through these before actually going out because you're too late when the urge hits, and you don't have a strategy!

You can change habits without logging, but a log just increases your chances of success, and why wouldn't you want to do that? Things are hard enough without making use of all the tools available to you. A log will help you to excel, as it encourages you to be consistent. It makes you aware of what you really are doing. It motivates you because, in that file, you want to write good stuff. It helps to hold you accountable before the people to whom you committed.

That is the key to changing habits. Every habit has at least one cause— an occurrence that goes immediately before the habit. Most habits have more than one cause— my causes included waking up, eating, sex, stressful events, going out drinking, etc., for example, when I drank. I would smoke almost without fail each time these events happened— either that I would get the urge to do so.

The more coherent the relation to the cause, the greater the habit. So, when you try to break a habit, you need to learn all of the triggers (log it for a few days) and then create a positive habit to substitute each of the triggers with the bad habits. For example, running replaced smoking when I became stressed out. You need a catalyst for positive change of habit, such as exercise, that will happen every day (or as often as you need it to happen). For the workout, you can exercise right after your morning coffee (if you already have coffee every day at the same time) or right after work, if you get off work every day at the same time. Bring the triggers into your written plan and be very consistent with them — do the practice instantly, every time, when the triggers occur. The less you're compliant with your causes, the worse the habit will be.

With every change of habit, I find it important to read about it, before and during as much as possible. I'm going to do my research to find success methods, future challenges, good tools to help me succeed. And during the change of habit, I'll always read about in — blogs, newspapers, books, forums, success stories— to help motivate me. 11. Too early to change focus. Often, we're going to start a change of habit and turn our attention to something else within a week or two. Okay, by then, the habit is still not deeply entrenched, and so we've spent all that time trying to form a new habit and then lose it before it's on autopilot.

Stick to this routine for at least 30 days, instead, and be consistent as much as possible. Not clear. I mentioned this a couple of times now, but it should be dealt with because it is important. If you attach a habit to a trigger, you have to make that habit each time, immediately after the trigger. Sometimes, if you do it, and not others, you won't get a habit. Whenever possible, try not to miss a single time, because once you miss one time, you will be tempted to miss another time, and then a third time, and then you have nothing.

But do not give up whether you miss once, or twice, or three times. Just find out why you failed and prepare next time to overcome the hurdle. Then from then on, be as consistent as possible, until the habit is ingrained. If you quit, you let beat you by the failure. But if you reset your resolve, and learn from your failure, then the failure will be a positive thing that will help you succeed. As I said earlier, I see failure as a step toward success

1.4 Point to Ponder Altering Habits Switcher

The first technique is not to attempt to create a complete habit but to slip into it without effort. Let's say that every day you wish to meditate, instead of setting aside 20 minutes and a room for your new habit of meditation. Slip inside. When you get out of bed, just pause for a few seconds and look out for your breath. That is, it, just a couple of seconds. That's so simple that you'll barely notice the habit. Don't try to be the best meditator in the world, don't try to master the habit, just do some seconds of it, and get on with your day. Start doing it for 30 seconds, then a minute after that is something you do without thinking about it. But don't jump into that, just take a week or two before you get older. It seems ludicrously easy. For exercise, you can try the same thing— instead of going to the gym or doing a 30-minute run, just try push up when you're about to take a break from your computer — one push up. And try to do a plank just for 10 seconds while you watch TV.

Using Your Mobile This one is a version of Slipping into the Habit. But it benefits from how often we check our phones. Simple and obvious: place a photo with a message on the lock screen of your phone.

For instance, put a message on your lock screen, which says, "Breath." Or maybe "Get fit." Slip into your new habit when you check your phone and note this post.

If the phone says "Breathe," then just take a few seconds to pay attention to your breath. If it's saying, "Get fit," just do a push up or something like that. Obviously, you can't do that every time you look at your camera, but if you do it a couple of times a day, you'll fall easily into a new habit, and then you'll be in right direction to a healthy habit that could change your life. Changing habits is closely related to walking home through fresh snow. The very first person who crosses the snow must find a way through the snow, but others are going to follow that path, and it's getting easier and more comfortable. It's a matter of forging that initial path to form a habit until it's harder not to take it. Who wants to forge a new snow path? But let's take that idea a little further: what if you engineered it so that even the initial individual who forges through the snow would instead take that path than another because it would be easier not to take that path.

Engineer the habit to shift, so it's more difficult not to shape the habit. Why did habit changes fail? I think I can safely say that we all tried and didn't create a new habit or change an old habit at a few points in our lives, changing old ways and creating new ones can be challenging. The thing is, it can be difficult to create a new habit. Rationale: constructive reviews. Negative feedback is when our acts make us feel unsatisfied, uncomfortable, or unpleasant, or we get criticized, or we get a bad feeling rather than a positive one in some other way. For example, tough exercise involves inherent negative feedback since it is harder than sitting on the couch. Quitting smoking has negative feedback because you are feeling discomfort and impulses to quit.

Positive feedback, on the other hand, is that you look thinner or healthier when you get compliments from friends and family or the satisfaction from the number decreasing on the scale.

When you accomplish something big it is a great feeling Yet, particularly in the first few weeks, when the negative feedback makes it difficult to change your actions, habit reduction often fails. That's because, because of the negative feedback, it's easier to quit the change of habit than keep on making the new habit. Having a cigarette puff is better than enduring withdrawal pains. Sitting in living area eating fries and donuts is easier than walking out for that run. Changes in habit fail because the negative feedback from making the new habit outweighs the positive feedback, and not making the habit becomes easier. The habit change engineer So how do we get over this problem? Put yourself in the shoe of engineer

If negative feedback outweighs positive feedback, change of behaviour fails. Positive feedback has to outweigh negative feedback for making the behaviour change successfully. The solution: boost positive feedback and/or decrease negative feedback until the ratio prefers behavioural change. Think differently: if you want to take a certain path in the snow, put barriers along all the other paths, so it's hard to go somewhere, but the path you want to take is shovelled, so it's easy to follow that path. You should make changes in your routine, so it's easier to leave than making the habit. How to do it in your custom engineering solution, you have four choices. I'll give you some suggestions in each, but you'll have to come up with your own ideas to fit in with whatever pattern you're trying to change.

Many activities provide positive feedback immediately, but positive feedback is often delayed. Losing weight takes a while. It takes a while to get positive feedback from your blog. Not timely response in positive feedback is what causes many people to fail, as they don't get any positive feedback in the critical first few weeks. Alternatively, find ways to get positive feedback instantaneously.

The better, the more. To maximize chances of success, add as many of these (and others you may think of) as possible. You want to make it difficult not to practice that habit. As complicated as humanly possible. So, to do that, you need to put on yourself all sorts of negative feedback for not making the habit. When you enter a forum or a real-world community, or send people you know about regular updates, or update your blog followers, you'll face the shame of telling people that you haven't questioned them. Get a partner or coach or coach, or your spouse, to make sure you're making that habit, and nag you if you don't. Delete all other temptations if you are trying to develop the reading habit. If you're trying to work out, get rid of television and the Internet and make your house noisy until you do your workout. Once you've been exercising, get your cable TV box or internet modem back from your neighbour who kept it for you. If you are trying to quit smoking, tell your children not to smoke. I'm sure there are many others you might think of — be imaginative!

Positive feedback for not doing the activity reduces. What are your temptations today not to exercise your habit? Give some thought to this, then bring those positive things down. Few ideas: • If you're trying to exercise (a common example), you often get positive feedback from not exercising, so staying at home is relaxing. So it reduces relaxation at home if that's the case. Have your spouse or children nag you. Go and call your wife. Remove cushions from the sofa. Let's be creative! If you are trying to stop procrastination, the positive feedback for procrastination is the pleasure of going on the Internet (for example). Okay, disconnect from the Internet, or use a device to block time-wasting websites.

If you're trying to wake up early, the positive feedback that comes from sleeping in is, of course, there. Set up alarms across your room.

Let people make wake-up calls to you, so you can't sleep. Have people waiting for you at the morning run track or waiting for an early business call from your phone.

How to Turn Your Goals into Habits It's such a simple concept, and yet it's not always something we do. It's not exceedingly hard to do, and yet I think it's something that would make anybody's life a world of difference. Bring your goals into habits and focus on auto-piloting those habits. There may be number of questions about focusing on One Goal is much more important than setting multiple targets. There were questions about my personal goals (like running a marathon, debt reduction, etc.) and how I could achieve them when working on different projects, and so on. How can you achieve one goal that takes a long time while still working on smaller projects at the same time?

These are excellent questions, and my response takes a little bit of explanation: I strive to turn my goals into behaviours, and I place my goals on autopilot in doing so. Turning a target into a habit just means focusing on it, constantly, to the exclusion of all else for at least a month.

The more you can concentrate on that, the more autopilot it will be. But once you activate it on autopilot mode, once a routine is firmly established, you really don't have to think about it much. You're always going to do it, but because it's a routine, you just have to use limited attention to keep the habit going.

The goal becomes autopilot, and you can concentrate on your next goal, project, or habit. Let's take an example of my Marathon goal. I had just started running, and within a year, I had the brilliant idea of running a marathon. (Btw, that's not the brightest idea — you're supposed to run for a couple of years before you try marathon training, or it's going to be much, much harder for you.) So that was my target, and it was my primary focus for some time.

Yet I broke it down into two habits for achieving that goal: I had to make a daily habit of running (while following an online training schedule I found). In order to be accountable, I had to report to people— I did every two weeks by family, friends, and colleagues, a blog, and a column to my local newspaper. There's no way that I would stop running with this responsibility. It took around a month to develop a daily running habit. I focused exclusively on this for about a month and had no other ambitions, tasks, or behaviours that were my primary. I've done other work projects, but they kind of needed a running backburner. It took some time for the responsibility habit, probably because I was not concentrating too much on that while I was forming the jogging habit, but it stuck, and for that first year of jogging/running, I'd chat about my running to people I met and blog every day (this was in blogger community that has since been deleted), and I'd write a column every two weeks for my local paper.

Once those two habits had been firmly entrenched, my goal for the marathon was pretty much on autopilot. I could focus (as an example) on my debt reduction goal, without having to worry too much about the marathon. Of course, I still had to do the job, but it didn't necessitate constant focus. I ran the marathon in the end. It was able to accomplish because all year round, I had the daily routine and regular habit of obligation. I put my marathon goal on autopilot, and that made it much easier — instead of dealing with it for a whole year every day, I focused on it for a month (well, really two) and was able to accomplish it while focusing on new habits and goals.

Other Applications Naturally, this works for many other types of goals. For instance:

- **Debt reduction**: I have converted this objective into a few different habits, including developing a monthly spending plan, learning to adhere to the spending plan, and making automatic debt and savings payments.

- **Weight loss**: An important first step was daily exercise patterns. Instead, I got to eating healthier habits, one at a time. I've recently added the habit of tracking my calories, and that's really helped.

- **Writing**: This was just setting the time to write, and making me write, no matter what. Once you've got the habit, the book comes in.

- **Getting organized**: these are three key behaviours — designating a spot for everything I own, immediately putting items in their designated spots, and checking your inbox(s) on daily basis.

As you can see, if you think through it just about any target can be turned into habits. Let's dig more into how this should be done. How to Turn A Target into Habits It's a very simple process, but let's step-by-step go about it: 1. Your goal should be very clearly written down. The more the target can be visualized, the easier it will be. Think of the steps you need to get to your target. There could be others. Can a series of daily or weekly actions accomplish the goal? For example, you will need to make a savings deposit will payday before you pay your bills, to save money. The goal will eventually be accomplished through that regular action. Work this out, and that's your pattern or collection of customs.

Figure the amount of habit that will have to be done by your timeline to get you to your goal. By "number," I mean, you need to find out the frequency of the quantity times to get your desired result.

For example, if I don't do enough miles or long runs, I can run every single day but aren't prepared to run a marathon. So, if I run every day, I need to know how far (and any other stuff like different workouts on different days) too. If I have a savings deposit every week, I need to know how much is needed for each deposit to reach my goal.

For your habit, find out this "number" and make a schedule. Spend at least one month on the first pattern, to the exclusion of all else. Don't think (for example) about the other two habits while you're trying to form the first habit. This book is a good place to start for more on habit formation. If more than one habit is required, start with the second habit after about a month, then with the third habit, and so on, concentrating on one habit at a time until each one is firmly entrenched. After getting acquainted with all the requisite behaviours, your target is on autopilot. You'll still need to reflect on them a little bit but to a lesser degree. If any of the habits are broken, you will need to focus on that habit again for a month. Once autopilot mode is activated, you can focus on a new target and set of habits

Chapter 2: Habits Switcher for Better Mind and Physical Fitness

First thing in the morning, drink a glass of water. Often, we don't get enough water in our systems and get so busy all day long that we don't care about stopping to fill up our supply. Or we fill up with soda or coffee or tea but not with water. Trigger by putting a large glass out on the counter or table. Or do what I do, with a lid, and get a big travel mug. At night, I fill it up with a lot of ice and some water, and it's waiting for me in the morning: a beautiful, refreshing cup of water. Flush the poisons, kick-start the body and wake up. Par as far away from the door as you can. Combat the consequences of a sedentary lifestyle whenever you can by incorporating more moves into your day. In reality, simple things like a long walk from the car to the door could be more successful than a hard workout to mitigate the long-hour effects at a desk. Eat every meal with raw fruits or vegetables. Think a green side salad, a slice of melon, some tomatoes, a couple of carrot sticks and slices of cucumber. You will not only get more nutrients in, but you will also get more fiber and potentially help your body lose weight, retain energy, and reduce hunger.

2.1 Physical Activity

Stand up and stretch out on the hour, every hour. Trigger yourself on your phone with a beep or watch (do people still wear those?) or a device. Sitting for more extended periods is a bad idea for your body as well as your brain. You need a physical and mental break, and that doesn't have to be a big deal. Only stop when your beep sounds at you on-the-hour. Stand wherever you are, reach over your head, breathe deeply, touch your toes, roll your shoulders. Carry a small nut bag or beef jerky wherever you go.

There's something protein-rich that will help stave off hunger and keep you from getting to that ravenous point when you're going to eat anything in sight, no matter what the calories count. Having a little extra protein in your diet will help boost your metabolism as well as develop your muscles. Ask open-ended questions. Ask bigger, better questions instead of tossing out items so that you can inject your view. Do not ask questions that have the answer with a simple Yes or No. Try out problems starting with "What do you think...?"And" How are you going to? "And" What is the case with you...?"Look at the answers than with the attitude you are here to learn. Having a clear perspective and initiating more in-depth conversations will help you relate to others, foster empathy, keep your issues in perspective, make new friends, and learn new ways to approach life. Imagine the insight you'd acquire in five or ten years if you just had one of these weekly conversations.

Hold your table/desk/shelf with a tray of art supplies out. Don't force yourself or even expect to clock in some minutes or productions. Just keep them out, in reach, so it's effortless when you feel like doodling something artistic around. Bonus points: turn the art medium out every week or month (pastels, crayons, aquarelles, paint, clay, playdough, knife carving & block wood). Sit back in silence every day for a few minutes. We don't need to call this meditation, because it could be a bit too intimidating. You don't need to lie with your legs crossed. You don't have to turn a blind eye. You don't have to be in anyway zen-like. Your brain may fly a hundred miles an hour, but do not say anything or do anything. Just sit comfortably and take a few minutes to breathe.

Jot down everything on your mind at the end of the day for a couple of minutes an as easy as a brain dump as possible. It might feel like a daily newspaper, or to-dodo list or planner isn't a big deal.

Keep a small bedside diary and allow yourself a few minutes before you go to sleep to pour out all that is on your mind. Don't edit them. Let it all stand out in any order, in any format. Even to you, it doesn't have to make sense. Studies show that writing of this sort can lower anxiety and depression. Alternative: use a voice recorder and simply talk into your microphone for a few minutes in an unedited stream-of-consciousness format. When you hit stress points, repeat a personal mantra to yourself. Make it simple to consider something that calms you down and reminds you of the essential things in life. This is an easy way of retraining the brain and telling it how to respond to stress. Instead of allowing stressful points to send you into a panicked mode, you're pulling out your mantra and telling your brain it's okay. Some of my favourites: that's going to happen too. I'm better than I had imagined. When I need to learn that, I can learn what I need to learn. I have done worse than that. I'm not alone on this. Freedom is here. I take power when I shoulder responsibility.

2.2 Habits Switcher for Good Job and Performance

Pretend your hero. Think about a hero in your industry or career when you are faced with a challenging situation, an intimidating project, a new career leap, an important meet. Then ask yourself what that person in your situation would do. How did she cope with this? Would he have been bullied? Mind-shaking '? So, rest assured, so rest assured? Just imagine what you think you'd do. It helps clarify what the right actions are for you, by eliminating the self-doubt and negative self-talk that can bog you off in confusion. Do a5-minute routine end-of-day analysis at your office. It takes five minutes before you leave the job, or at home from your office before you wrap things up for the day (or night!).

In a fast, bulleted list, write down what you've accomplished. Write down what you have not done and what you have wished for, and what has hindered you. Don't beat yourself up for your mistakes; just remember what caused you to get off track if you can. And remember how much you did. This form of analysis is a way to help the brain concentrate on the positive (I've achieved something today) and help you become more mindful of the things that tend to disrupt you or distract you from productive work.

Switch off all updates daily for at least one long block of working time. The brains are not able to move from task to task. Even if it's about something completely unimportant, the single ding of an email notification or text will cause you to lose up to 40 percent of your work time. Is it worth it, really? So, if you have an endless amount of time at your fingertips. But we all know you don't. So, do yourself and your career a favour, and for at least one long block of time (2–4 hours), silence all the dings and chirps. Respond with "I'll check my calendar" for all invites and opportunities. Stop the knee-jerk reaction you send, whether it's negative or positive. You may be too fast to say no (I am). Or perhaps you're a people-pleaser and too quick to say yes, and you're overbooked and exhausted. Give yourself time to evaluate every opportunity, simply by making it your practice not to respond immediately. Alternatively, say, "I'm going to check my calendar and let you know." So, when you've got a little time, check your schedule, your goals and decide what you can fit into it.

Spend 5 minutes a day thinking about the steps that you're going to take to get you to your career goals. This is the most appropriate kind of positive visualization. Visualizing the end result usually doesn't help you get there. Yet visualizing yourself doing the steps you're going to take to achieve your ultimate goal will help you pursue these steps when it's time.

2.3 Little Better Relationship Habits

Call, send, or email one friend or member of your family a day. Staying in touch has never been easier, but only communicating with the people we see at work or those who just won't stop appearing on our Facebook feed is all too easy. Reach out to stay connected with the friends and family members you love a little bit more. Investing in a relationship takes just a few minutes, resulting in you having a strong network of people around you, near and far. Each week write down a thank you note. For you alone, this can be an exercise: write a thank-you letter to someone who has been passed away but has had an impact on your life and tell them all the things you wish you could do. Or write a thank you note to someone who is or has been part of your life and send it to that person. Cultivating gratitude helps loosen your life's fear. How much different would your life be if you had been teaching yourself to be appreciative rather than fearful?

End the night with a word of gratitude or encouragement. This is the sort of simple habit that a lifelong relationship can make or break. Before you go to sleep and roll over, let your significant other know that you accept him and value him or her. You don't need to be elaborate: "I love to be with you," or "Thank you for being there for me," send the right message. If you are not in a relationship, say a word of thanks or motivation to yourself. Sounds stupid? Perhaps. But it can help build confidence and keep you from spiralling into depression one bad day.

Pause before answering or answering people. Train yourself to listen well, not while the other person is talking, by giving yourself time to think through your answer in that pause.

This not only shows you trust what the other person says (which expresses approval and respect), but it also gives you time to weigh up your attitude and vocabulary. A simple five-second pause in a high-tension situation or stressful conversation could be what keeps you from blowing up and running a relationship you value.

Give yourself some time off. Everything is happening. If you feel stressed, irritated, angry, or impatient, you will hit points. That's all right, because if you can take a time-out, then you can keep things in perspective. You cannot expect to be a non-emotional robot, but when things get to you, you can train yourself to take a seven-minute break from humanity. Walk around the block, lock yourself in the bathroom, take a quick drive down with the windows, and the blaring music. Find and use the "time-out chair" that works for you.

Few environments for a better environment and society. Take a short walk with a trash bag around the block and pick up litter. This weekly or daily ritual will help you become more aware of how you treat your everyday environment, and you never know what effect it can have on others. Sometimes just one person takes the time to make something better can also spark others to take care of things better.

Arrange and say hello to your neighbours. Make it a habit of doing more than just a nod or a smile. It only takes a moment to step over and say hello, whenever you see them out. Create a more friendly community, and also help the people around you get plugged in. Some of my best friends are neighbours interested in learning over the fence and chatting for a minute. Now they're the ones calling to see if I need anything while they go to the supermarket or offering to babysit to my children if I don't feel good. Borrow for big purchases before you buy.

It can't always be, but why not try it? Save energy and assist the community.

Consider it a habit to borrow first, check it out, and see if it is what you need / want / must-have. Then try buying used before purchasing new. This will obviously not apply to every big purchase. But it will apply to a lot.

Set aside gift money. It might just be a small amount. Ultimately. Five dollars will make a great difference for someone. Put aside a small bit of each pay check, or the total income of each month, forgiving. It has to be no-strings-attached and, where possible, anonymous is the way to go. Aid the neighbours. Donate yourself to charity. Buy a meal for that homeless guy. All of us are a part of the same human family. Hold out your bike where you can see it. No, you don't have to use it. Just put it in front of you, where you can have its eyeball. When you sprint to the car every day and climb in. Wait, don't you have a motorbike? Hmmm, hmmm. Perhaps call up a neighbour to see if you can borrow one.

2.4 Plan Your Day Throughout the Year

Plan your day Throughout the years, I felt frustrated and unproductive if I didn't follow this advice. I slowly discovered that organizing and implementing a schedule can make a huge difference in how I feel and what I am doing. Here are some of the things that help me to manage my schedule so you might find it helpful: a) Create a routine No matter what you're working on, create a routine. Blocking times for specific activities and keeping to the plan. Turn your calendar into a bunch of blocks and put those blocks into the activities. You don't do whatever isn't expected.

If you want to have free time, plan it out. Your schedule may change throughout the year, but it's best to have a plan at any given time. For example, if you are working on starting a business and need to find, code, and recruit customers, then set priorities and block specific times for each task.

A calendar app is a very helpful resource b) Team meetings and calls into blocks. For example, if you need to have external meetings, block those meetings two and a half days a week, and only go to the external meetings during those hours. Do the same for meetings held in-office. This means you're not just making a chunk of time for meetings; you're also creating other time blocks that you're going to be able to do important work. Do the same with calls, and book them all back and forth.

Optimize the time for different types of meetings. Personally, I'm a big fan of 30-minute meetings and 10-minute calls now. I think 10-minute calls are a great way to connect with someone at first or give quick advice to someone. If you prefer to see the person, you can do a Google Hangout or Skype, rather than just hear them. The reason the calls work for 10 minutes is that people skip BS and get to the point. Give it a try. Ten minutes, if you concentrate, is really a lot of time. I'd rather make those calls on Fridays when I usually work from home. I am not a big fan of coffee introductions, lunches, and dinners. I'm a huge coffee and meal fan with people that I already know. These meetings are typically productive and fun, but it is more productive to do a call or an actual 30-minute meeting in the office when you meet someone for the first time. Here are the types of meetings you might want to book:

- A 20-minute meeting in the office to get to know or catch up with someone outside the office • 45-minute meeting. Allow traveling for 15 minutes.

- A 10-minute call to support those seeking guidance

- 15-minute daily stand-up — perfect for start-ups and engineering teams

- 30-minute weekly staff meeting Any meetings you have, divide them into blocks according to your schedule.

If you feel you need time for a particular type of meeting, then adjust the block accordingly.

Use Appointment Slots Google Calendar has a great feature called Appointment Slots. It lets you book a chunk of time, and then break it into bits. I may book three hours of outside meetings, for example, and then split it into three meetings — one hour each. Or I can book one hour of calls and break it into six calls every 10 minutes.

There's also a bunch of specific tools that do that, like doodle, too. The next move is to build bit.ly links for different time periods. You can have a connection for your external meetings, another link for 30-minute meetings within, and another for 10-minute calls. You then share these links, and they will be able to book your time. I've done this with candidate companies from TechStars, and it has been incredibly effective.

This simplified email back and forth, which saved me and the businesses a ton of time. This isn't going to work with everyone, because some people might find that rude. In any case, if you don't feel comfortable giving someone the connection, then you can use your own appointment slots, suggest a few meeting times, and then book the actual slot for yourself. When you ask someone to meet, always suggest multiple different alternate times e) Block email time. This is the most important tip in the entire post. Email is your property unless you own it. You must avoid doing so all the time to own your email.

You must arrange the time to do your email to do that. It's absolutely a must that I get 300 to 400 emails per day for TechStars (all of which I answer) and perhaps 50 to 70 personal emails (mostly spam). Many tech-workers are like me. We just love sweets because they're short, but they're not emails. What they are is stress.

The stress isn't caused by the sheer volume of emails, though. It's caused by the chaotic way we process them typically, and by the fact that new emails arrive while we respond to existing ones. Here's a system that's incredibly simple but can probably dramatically reduce the amount of time you're spending on the email along with the stress it causes you.

Install the extension Gmail Inbox Pause. If you don't use Gmail, then start using it, get this extension. Adopt a system for labelling.

- Fast emails: can be managed in less than 30 seconds

- Garbage emails: can only be removed on line

- Important emails: take time and need to be answered regularly

- Other emails: less important emails that need not be answered frequently Block the corresponding time slots in your calendar. Monday, Wednesday, Friday and Sunday: one hour to scan emails, respond quick ones, remove garbage ones and mark the rest

- Monday, Wednesday and Sunday: one hour after the above hour to reply to emails labelled essential

- Friday: one hour after the hour of fast emails to reply to emails labelled another Press pause, sit back and relax. If you're getting bored, go read Entrepreneur.com or Tweets. I'd rather work, When the email scanning reminders arrive, hit uncaused. Load all new emails, and you go one hour through them. You answer quick ones, delete some of the garbage and then name the rest. My scanning time is 2-3 p.m. Of course, you can do this anytime, but I like to keep the mornings clean and free of emails. Move back to step four, when you're done.

It's important to stack the times as I did above because if you don't have a ton of new emails, you get to important ones quicker, so you will get some free time for yourself.

When one hour isn't enough, continue adding 30 minutes to each location? It really should be enough because you're focused solely on the emails. Set the rule during this period that you're busy, and view this as a meeting you can't get out of. Note that you won't see your mobile phone emails either. Clearly, the whole system fails if you do it all the time. Pausing is super important as it reduces stress absolutely. I try to avoid leading emails.

Plan your exercise and your family time. Unless you put it on the calendar, it's not going to happen. Well, that's true of your exercise and your family's time. Whether you're going in the morning, afternoon, or evening, you're doing it three times a week or every day, put your workout time on the calendar. My friend and mentor, Nicole Glares, makes it very clear that she belongs to her days before 10 a.m. Depending on the weather, she hits the pavement or the gym, and she rarely deviates from her routine. The same goes for spending time with your family and other significant ones. If you're a workaholic like me, you'll end up stealing time from your family unless you book it beforehand and train yourself to unplug it promptly. Many people in the industry have been talking about family time planning. My favourite is Brad Feld, who speaks a lot about it.

I think about my time a lot manage your time. I'm thinking about where that is going. I'm curious about where I can get more and how to maximize it. I had an assistant who managed my time when I was running Get Glue. She was terrific.

But when I joined TechStars, I decided I was going to manage my own calendar. I must admit I am happy with this decision. I think about what I'm doing, who I'm meeting with, and why a lot more. I get to meet a lot of people every week. My timeline during the selection process is especially crazy.

And I find myself less distracted and less depressed as I monitor my schedule, follow a routine, arrange meetings in blocks, and use appointment slots. Owning my calendar and organizing my days and weeks made me a happier, more productive human being. I hope this post will help you get to that point too.

Chapter 3: Habits Switcher for professionals

Few Professional Habits Leading a team can be stimulating, gratifying, and draining. Busy working conditions can give team leaders little time to check-in with team members to make sure they feel comfortable, innovative, and on track. But there's an alternative with these six simple and effective Team Management tips. How to achieve Successful Team Management with effective channels of communication and plenty of input opportunities, you can provide a strong support system for your team. With this, team leaders can develop transparency, trust, and a less hierarchical approach. Here are our few tips on creating a happier and more productive team through some positive workflows:

3.1 Be Open.

It has been found that transparent working environments make teams more accountable, productive, and innovative.

It sounds like a big claim, but open environments help develop a sense of mutual respect among team members and team leaders. Transparent and authentic workplaces help employees feel secure in their positions through clear and consistent communication. Team members, in effect, feel freer to add ideas and suggestions and to increase creativity.

Most senior professionals agree that workplace accountability is vitally important.

Professional describes how they use openness in their business for effective team management: "How can the company learn, evolve and thrive if people are afraid to be themselves, voice their opinions and show sincerity that they care about the brand and the team? Making the business become a sort of safe space helps brilliant ideas to flourish and issues to be highlighted and discussed head-on in the organization. "Professional and his team aim to make all employees feel, respected and valued in the loop. Consequently, they found that each member of the team was more secure in their work, but also more imaginative and loyal.

Intuitive task management James Hanna, the team management expert, uses straightforward tools to accept that accountability is a pillar in high-functioning teams. James states that teams use Mistreats to attain effective team and project management in their projects. You do this by presenting team members with a summary of tasks and roles through their mutual project boards: "If all the team members can have a high level of visibility over the project while also recognizing the role you play at any given time, you can foster a sense of obligation and build transparency amongst team members." This also helps team members to understand their role within the larger picture. With all roles and responsibilities transparently shown, team leaders may take a less hands-on approach, realizing the assigned individual can interpret each task through.

3.2 Keep Communicating

You must have learned this before: Good communication is the foundation of a cohesive and successful team.

The aim is to create an ambiance where team leaders feel able to provide truthful and constructive input, and team members feel confident about voicing concerns and engaging with each other. Google Hangouts can provide an ideal way for teams of members working remotely to ensure a certain amount of face-to-face time is accomplished. If your dispersed team is working through time zones and you'd like to set up a standing appointment for calls, finding a time that works for everyone involved is important. By not always keeping calls to a remote team member at inconvenient times, they will be more available (and awake) to connect with you frankly and accurately. Use a chat channel, like Slack. Slack is another great communication device. Various companies are already using software like Slack, as it's a perfect way to cut down on communications and build a positive and enjoyable working culture irrespective of whether the team works remotely or all in one office. We have a' stand up' Slack channel at Meiselas, where everyone begins their day by discussing what they're going to work on. It helps avoid siphoning between departments and gives administrators a good idea of what everybody's priority will be for. It also encourages team members to step in when it is necessary and offer support.

Providing valuable feedback, It is one of the best ways you can help team members to improve professionally and personally. Jean-François Manzoni, IMD International's Professor of Leadership and Organizational Development, explains: "You're doing your star a disservice if you don't help her find out how she can keep growing." Even if you don't have any negative feedback, make sure you have daily check-in opportunities.

That way, you can give advice on how you feel that your team members are improving and can develop even further. Such conversations also provide a good opportunity to share your constructive feedback if there are any areas of work that you believe could be strengthened.

Feedback can be intimidating but an essential part of effective team management. When summarizing her advice on how to provide successful feedback, Belle Beth Cooper said: "If you find a challenging or nervous conversation, remember that your purpose in providing feedback is to help your team members thrive and grow." Therefore, while feedback conversations can be difficult, particularly in non-hierarchical organizations, they are important and necessary for tea growth.

Encourage teamwork Inevitably; if your team members can get along well with each other, they'll be happier. These will also perform better, as an added bonus. Foster collaboration among your team members to accomplish tasks means there's potentially a whole host of varied talents on your squad. Make sure the use of these various skillsets means that everyone is aware of ongoing projects. Therefore, team members should hop into work anywhere they believe interest can be given. For example, I will often rely on the expertise of the SEO expert on our marketing team when designing the content strategy. Similarly, if I learn that the SEO expert is coming up with text for a PPC campaign, I'll be offering help. A collaborative task management tool will assist in this step by communicating with the rest of your team the upcoming tasks for each team member. Use software like Google Drive Collaboration has been found to increase innovation, so resources like Google Drive, which allow you to update shared documents in real-time while you are working, are perfect.

Within our marketing team, we use the upload function of Google Docs within Mistreats to share documents via the task in question. It means we are always working on the document's most up-to-date version; as other members of the team will update it in real-time.

We then use the function of commenting on each task to leave relevant feedback, questions, or updates on how the task is to evolve. Start planning out your thoughts. Consider using a collaborative online mind map for a less linear perspective on collaborative working. Many users can access mind maps at the same time with Mideastern, meaning team members can add their suggestions, give feedback, or vote on ideas up or down. All of this can be achieved in real-time, whether it's brainstorming together in a group or operating remotely. Collaboratively generating ideas while mind mapping was found to improve creative thinking, since it combines both linear, convergent (left-brain) thinking and divergent, non-linear (right-brain) thinking. It involves the whole mind in the development and creation of new information, using our visual, auditory, and kinaesthetic senses to develop new concepts and stimulate our imaginations.

Delegating tasks. As I asked the multiple CEOs what his recommendation would be for other team leaders, he said it would be to always know when to delegate tasks. Companies hire competent staff for a reason, and micro-management should not mean effective team management. If you have recruited staff for a specialized field such as programming, you need to know when to leave them to do their work. Delegate tasks while staying in the loop Sometimes, it can be difficult to let go.

Especially if you have been working on a project for some time but need a member of the team to take it over, try using the Watching feature with Mistreats, where you can attach yourself as a watcher.

Becoming a 'watcher' lets you stay in the loop with the progress of the mission and any associated discussions. Michael Krannert, Meiselas ' Growth Marketer, explains how this role helps him to efficiently run the Growth Team here at Meiselas: "At each point, the project task is allocated to a specific person... Other team members will" watch "the progress of the test, keeping everyone in the loop with how the experiment is progressing... As experiments grow, we shift the tasks between the parts. All members of the team who "watch" the experiment is informed of the transfer.

By allowing "watchers" to keep an eye on development, the feature allows team leaders to entrust team members to follow their tasks or projects on their own while feeling able to jump in to inquire or support where it's useful. Keep an overview of team progress and project progress. In Mistreats, team members can get a clear overview of team progress and task progress through the Statistics & Reports section. Team efficiency can be viewed transparently, with graphs on task development and completion, and reports can be downloaded as CSV files if needed. Teams may also choose to chart their activities in time to gain even more insight into how long projects take.

Active task management 6. Prevent team burn-out. You're in a great position as a team leader to set positive work, play, and relaxation boundaries. In an essay on handling job alerts, managers are responsible for setting the standard as to when and where team members will turn off completely from work. This could mean, for example, by not expecting team members to check emails after working hours. That can be challenging, of course. Particularly in teams where members are versatile in their work and may choose to start early or work late, saving time elsewhere may not be keeping a work-life balance. Nonetheless, it is important to encourage team members to set some work limits, to sleep well, and to prevent burn-out.

You can choose which updates to receive using Mistreats and Slack, our main communication channels at Meiselas. For example, if I've been listed or sent a direct message, I'll only receive a Slack push notification on my laptop. Similarly, as Belle Beth Cooper suggests, team members can try to set up their phones, so they can switch off, relax, and rejuvenate when they finish the night.

3.3 Complete Your Hardest Task First

A "lizard" is that thing on your to-do list that is ugly, disgusting, that you want to put off more than anything else until later. It's something you need to do, but you've got absolutely zero drive to do it. If you have ten things to do and you put off the one thing you hate, then ultimately, it still needs to be done. But while you're doing the other nine things, the negative one pounds on your mind, drains your passion, zaps your inspiration, saps your strength, and makes you miserable in general. Contrary to this, if you do the hard things first, eat your ugly lizard for breakfast, the other tasks will fly by. You are freed from delay, freed from anxiety, and happy in all other endeavours. Reasons why you must first deal with a hideous lizard in the morning.

It builds momentum.

You know how amazing it feels when you tick your to-dodo list for a task, right? So, you all know it feels like even better when that task is the most difficult task that you have. It's kind of a relief! And the rest of the day's feeling like a breeze once it's out. And you don't spend the day in fear, so it's easier to be in a better mood and much more successful than that. First of all, doing the toughest job can create momentum in your day-and that can be the difference between one that is successful and one that is not.

Develop Positive Dependence. You may develop a "healthy addiction" to endorphins and to the feeling of enhanced clarity, trust, and ability they cause. Once you develop this addiction, you will begin to plan your life on an unconscious level in such a way that you are constantly beginning and completing ever more important tasks and projects. In a very positive sense, you'll become addicted to success and your contribution. Setting short and long-term smart goals will help you experience this "hooked" feeling as the pleasure of completing each task stimulates the reward and enjoyment function of the brain.

It feels great to get the ugly thing off your to-dodo list. This gives you a sense of accomplishment when you cross the nasty, awful thing off your to-dodo list and mark a count in the column of a small win. Even small wins can give you more willpower. Studies have shown that our pre-frontal cortex (the area of the brain which we use for willpower) will start firing neurons when we achieve a small win. When it does so, our concentration, perseverance, and ability to resist temptation increases. That essentially gives us "free" willpower throughout the day to use on other tasks.

It frees you up to the job you enjoy doing. Productive jobs are one of the keys to prosperity. When we talk about hating our jobs, the lizards really are what we are talking about! We talk about those things that we don't have the motivation to do. We are not talking about purposeful activities that help us at our craft to become better. Those are the activities which motivate us to do a great job! You get to spend the rest of the day doing the work that you enjoy doing by eating your lizard first thing in the morning. Secondly, the sort of job that has helped you choose your profession. By making this a habit, you will find much more contentment and happiness in your everyday work.

If you've got to eat a live lizard at all, sitting down and looking at it for a very long time doesn't pay. The key to achieving high performance and productivity levels is developing the lifelong habit of tackling your major task first thing every morning. Before doing anything else and without taking too much time to think about it, you must establish the routine of "eating your lizard" Among successful people, this practice is well-adopted by it is an essential quality of leadership for anyone who wants to achieve great things. The practice is the key to any skill you master. Fortunately, your mind is just like a muscle. It grows stronger and more user-friendly. You can learn any behaviour with practice or develop any habit you consider desirable or necessary. What is a "lizard? "What is the one thing you regularly despise? Once you've selected your "lizard," make it a habit of waking up every morning and doing that task first.

3.4 Break Down Your Big Goals into Smaller Goals

Inside your team and in your personal life, it's nice to have big goals to reach for. But if the distance between where you're standing right now and your goals is too big, you may be setting yourself to fail.

At first, ambitious goals are inspiring and motivating, but they can become intimidating unless they are accompanied by actionable steps toward how to reach them. That's why priorities need to be broken down into actionable tasks.

Goals need not only be achievable and desired but must be specific. Definitions are important to expectations since they make sure you visualize the desired outcome. Setting targets that aren't specific immediately reduces the chance you'll reach them. Why are You supposed to? You haven't mentioned when to reach that goal, or what the target really is.

Here are some examples of how specific you need to be:

• A man decides to lose weight after Christmas and writes it down. He weighs 10 pounds less by the middle of July but feels he has failed.

- A man makes it his target to lose 5 pounds a month before July. He sets down the exact diet and exercise regimen he must maintain to ensure he fulfils his goals. He's lost 30 lbs by mid-July. Even though he hasn't achieved every goal, he's found great success along the way and is motivated to keep getting in shape.

- A woman has a target of writing a novel within four months. Her first month is an extremely successful one. She's doing extensive-time period work and designing beautiful characters and writing an extremely rough draft. Yet life is getting crazy, so she's setting it aside and taking a break. The rugged draft is still untouched three months later.

- A woman decides to draw up a rigorous and regulated schedule of writing and breaks in order to write her novel within four months. She writes for 5 hours each day. She sets due dates for testing, writing, polishing, page numbers, and even talking to editors. Its habit soon forms, and the book is written.

It's easy to get excited when you set goals and start with gusto, but it's much harder to maintain stamina and enthusiasm for them in the long term. That's why the plans of the New Year usually die before February. Holding your goals clear and comprehensive will help keep you focused on the long haul. Of course, you need to have goals before you break down your goals into tasks. It's important to be as specific as they can for the targets you set. Let's take the example of running a marathon, as we have already talked about how much a start-up feels like. If your goal is to run a marathon, what exactly does that mean? Can you go marathon part? Would you like to finish in a given time? A scientific review of dietary and exercise behavioural changes shows that specific, challenging goals result in better performance than vague goals. This is very likely to apply to non-nutritional and physical exercise areas too. Get crystal clear about what you're trying to achieve, then write down. Goals would usually be broken down into milestones. Jog for thirty minutes, run 5k in thirty minutes, run a total weekly distance of 15k, run a total weekly distance of 25k. And so on. Milestones are still big steps, but they help you think about what you need to achieve your goals. You can start to grasp what's needed to reach each milestone and what you need to get there.

Now that you have a map of the milestones you want to accomplish, you can come up with a task list. You don't have to diagram your whole target. Begin with the first milestone and go there. If thirty minutes of jogging is your first goal, here's where you should continue. Buy running shoes, always start a nutrition plan and jog three times a week Make your tasks workable by starting them with a verb, and make sure that you are really clear about what each task involves. If any function is still unclear, then further break it down.

Try to anticipate if there's anything you need to complete each step before you start working away at each mission. You may need to set up a meeting with a nutritionist in our marathon example, or you may want to do some research on what the best running shoes are to you. It is even more critical within the workplace to find out what is needed to complete every task, as team members also rely on each other. When one team member lacks the ability to complete one mission, the entire team will be set back. Think of all the practical things that you will need to complete each task, whether it's knowledge or professional help. Start making plans beforehand to make sure when you need it, what you need will be there.

Once you've got your task list, it's time to create your task timeline. The timeline will enable you to see what needs to happen to get a task started, and what tasks can happen next to each other. But this is not about multitasking! For example, starting your nutrition plan and jogging three days a week will happen alongside each other, but first, you need to purchase your running shoes. Having a schedule for your activities will allow you to see your goals in a more realistic light and will also enable you to be more productive about how you spend time.

You have your goals, your milestones, and your duties. The big advantage of breaking down your goals into tasks is that it provides short, actionable, and realistic steps that you need to take. There is no doubt that you can accomplish every individual task, which gives you the confidence to move quickly towards your objective. But imagine standing at a mountain's foot and looking up at the distant summit. Looking up at the summit, you may feel overwhelmed by how much you need to go hiking. You might even begin to doubt if you can climb the mountain anyway. Now, if you look at the first base, where you're standing a few hundred meters above, getting there will probably feel a lot more realistic than climbing the mountain.

You break down what might seem impossible into a series of doable steps when you break down objectives into tasks. Sometimes at the top, you can take a peak, picture yourself there, remember why you want to get there first. Yet keep your eyes fixed on the next camp, and walk slowly toward it, knowing that's what's going to get you to the top.

Setting job goals is seen as one of the best ways to be more successful. They are easy to make, but often hard to see through. Today's community is filled with great apps for task management and how much to-dos for success. Here are some of our steps to help you set goals, and make sure you keep to them! Start by deciding what you'd like to accomplish. When it comes to achieving objectives, developing the goals should be the most basic and obvious activity. But this may be a process more in-depth than you realize. It's important to know yourself to be leading yourself. Ask yourself, "What exactly do I want? "The truth of the goals is that you have to accomplish it and make sure you're inspired to achieve it, either out of need or desire.

Do not expect perfection, but make your goals based on your personal performance (beat a personal time vs. winning the race). Be specific and to the point. Break them down into sub-goals. Make it challenge to prioritize and organize your goals. Make Challenging your goals. An over-challenging goal can de-motivate a person, and it's true that people avoid pain, change, and difficulty. Yet human beings still thrive on challenges, and if properly motivated, they can work harder for a daunting target. Challenging goals help us achieve better. When we understand the difficulty of a task, we take it more seriously, train for it, prepare for it, and push it harder to get there.

If an employer gives an employee a list of 6 activities to complete in 10 hours, they are likely to have them completed in 10 hours. Nevertheless, if an employer gives an employee a list of 10 tasks to be completed in 10 hours, only eight or even ten can be completed. This example relates directly to knowing and leading yourself. Comprehend how much that is too much. Burning yourself out will achieve nothing. But when it's too easy to do something, delete the target and aim for something that needs more commitment. You will find that you have more to do than you have known. That is one of the most important goal-setting principles. A target without a time limit is like a sentence without a timeline. If you add a deadline to a task, it adds a level of urgency and incentive that wasn't there before, immediately. The person setting the goal makes a mental handshake on himself with a set deadline. Dates are a means of transparency and a key part of setting goals successfully.

It is a smart idea to break your targets into subtasks in order to further clarify and make your objectives more precise. Some task management software gives you subtasks, but if you're just keeping track of your own on paper, shaping is still a great habit. Just as the more specific tasks make them more tangible, the creation of subtasks allows the target setter to take baby steps. Especially if you are setting longer-term goals, it can be difficult to think only in terms of the future. It will help you move towards each target by preparing subtasks or baby steps you will achieve each day. Try to break things down instead of trying to take a giant leap towards a daunting target. You'll be motivated with subtasks and find satisfaction by seeing your goals being accomplished little by little. Accountability is another area of setting goal that will help motivate. When you're making a goal, it's up to you to keep up with the dates and tasks you set. We are not all honestly strong enough to hold ourselves accountable. If your goal is to stop smoking cigarettes, then your good intentions may be overwhelmed by addiction. Having a friend or adviser to hold you accountable is often a wise decision. Tell it to friends or your trusted advisors next time you create a goal. Simply speaking it to someone else can help to cement it in your mind. With a partner to keep you on track and challenge your successes, you'll be more likely to keep track of yourself.

When you have reached a goal, don't miss a chance to celebrate the achievement. Giving yourself a pat on the back for the stuff you set your mind to will encourage your positive behaviour. The most common examples of that are anniversary and graduations. Small or large rewards and celebrations are suitable for a well-done job. So whether you've been smoke-free for ages or your start-up has made it the first million dollars, celebrate the goals you've made and check them out.

Chapter 4: Be less reactive and more proactive

We all encounter experiences in life when a negative emotion can temporarily overwhelm us, be it frustration, anxiety, nervousness, depression, or uncertainty. In these cases, the distinction between constructive versus reactive, optimistic versus uncertainty, and performance versus failure can be made by how we choose to "master the moment."

Here are ten ways of being less reactive in difficult situations, with excerpts from my other books, What is common in the mentioned tips is that they bring a constructive disruption to a negative state of mind or emotion. However, brief or long, these conscious interjections provide a psychological opening from which you can recalibrate and choose more motivating action. Such guidelines may not all apply to your specific situation. Just use what functions, and delete all the rest.

4.1 Tips to React Less

If you feel angry and upset with someone, take a deep breath and count slowly to fifteen before you say or do something you may regret later. In most cases, you'd have worked out a better way to communicate the issue by the time you reach ten, so you can eliminate, rather than intensify the issue. If, after counting to ten, you are still angry, take time out, if possible, and revisit the issue after you calm down.

When you feel adverse about someone's actions towards you, avoid jumping straight away to a negative conclusion. Instead, come up with multiple ways of looking at the situation before it responds. I may be tempted to think, for example, that my friend did not return my call because she is avoiding me, or I might consider the possibility that she has been busy.

When we stop personalizing the actions of other people, we will interpret their gestures more critically and reduce the potential for confusion. If you're dealing with a difficult adult, try to put yourself in the shoes of the challenging person, even for a moment, and complete the sentence: "It shouldn't be easy..." For instance: "My child is so resistant. The school and social pressures must not be easy to deal with. ".." "My boss is really strict. It should not be easy for upper-management to put such high expectations on her performance. "To be sure, empathic comments do not justify unacceptable behaviour. The idea is to note that people are doing what they are doing because of their own problems. So long as we are rational and considerate, others ' challenging actions reveal much more about them than they do about us.

When someone asks you to decide, you're not sure about, just buy time and say, "I'm going to think about it." This expression will raise the psychological pressure immediately and place you in better control of the situation. Whether it's a friend asking for a favour, a romantic interest seeking a date, or an extreme sales request, take the time you need to weigh the pros and cons of the situation and decide whether you want to discuss a different arrangement, or whether you're better off by saying "no." Put cold water on your face if you feel nervous and anxious, which stimulates the reflex of mammalian diving and automatically lowers the heart rate from 10 to 25 percent.

Getting fresh air and taking deep breaths off the diaphragm is also beneficial. Have a hot cup of decaffeinated green tea when you feel stressed. Research has shown that green tea contains theanine amino acid, which helps to reduce stress. Holding a warm cup of drink in your hand can also elevate your mood. Stop caffeinated drinks that can fuel your nervousness. Consider vigorous aerobic exercises if you feel scared or discouraged. Energetics.

The way we make use of our bodies greatly affects how we feel. As the saying goes-emotions control movement. When you feel your body's strength, so will your confidence rise.

Whether it's oversensitivity, unnecessary anxiety, or unhealthy rumination when you find yourself distracted in a way you know it's not good for you, use a strategy created by psychologist Eric Maisel and say to yourself: "I'm not strolling over this! "Distract yourself from positive tasks so as not to be trapped. To maintain objectivity, ask for feedback from trusted colleagues and reliable advisors. If you're tired, frustrated, or uninspired, go into nature and cover yourself in green and blue colours that have a soothing effect. Take a panoramic view and look in the distance. Continue walking. Take breaths deeply. Immerse yourself in the splendour of nature. Come back with new ideas and a fresh perspective. Ask if you are going through setbacks and failures: "What is the lesson here? "From this experience, how can I learn? "What's the most important thing now? "And" When I think outside the box, what better answers are there? "The higher the quality of the questions that we pose, the greater the quality of the responses that we get. Ask insightful learning-based questions and goals, and we can get the right perspective to help us address the current situation.

4.2 Don't React What You See on Social Media

Social networking has revolutionized how people connect with friends and family members and has grown rapidly as a medium for marketing. Social networks can also cause procrastination, however. People spend hours scrolling through pictures and videos looking for communication, entertainment, and social status.

The question is too many social media when you continually turn to a paper writing service for help or have no time to care for yourself or have fun because you're too busy on social media. Keep on reading for tips on spending less time on social media.

Use social media marketing resources. If you need it to spread information about your company or a project, you're trying to start-up, it can be hard to stay away from social media. Consider using a social media marketing tool instead of visiting each site individually. One way to use these resources is to post them all over your pages at once. You also make it easy to track and respond to comments, answer messages, and manage the public image of your company. Working Away from Social Media There's nothing wrong with working on your new group project with colleagues or co-workers. Try taking the job off social media to remain successful. Collaborate on a forum for the exchange of information or get together at the library or somebody's home. There's no need to browse through social media for hours when you can just get the work done and not think about it. If you want to have fun, go out to celebrate, rather than going back home. Beat the Multi-Taking Habit When was your last impression of being a genius? Even though people think multi-tasking makes them work quicker, it slows them down. Speak of your brain as a Mac. Every time you turn to a new page, the more tabs you have open, the greater the lag. The brain needs time to adapt to new tasks, and it just isn't effective when you're switching back and forth.

Track Your Social Media Time. Do you really know how many hours you spend every day on social media? It can seem a little here, and there's not a big deal. At the end of the day, however, a few minutes here and there can add up to hours. Download an app that tracks time to watch how much time you spend each day on social media.

Then, try cutting back currently. You will decline a bit at a time. When you spend three hours, push yourself to cut back to 90 minutes each day. Then, from that, you can cut down more. Don't call it a punishment. Imagine how much more you can do in your newly found free time. Set a Social Media Calendar Setting a calendar is one way to cut back your time. Decide how many minutes you wish to commit to social media of your day. For example, at lunchtime, you might be spending 10-15 minutes and allowing yourself another 20 minutes after school or work. Set the alarm if you are having trouble keeping to the plan. Turn up and do another thing when it goes off. If you do something you love, it helps, but you should also get pleasure from your daily tasks. Unchain Yourself from all gadgets People are fascinated with social media because their cell phones permit continuous access. Nevertheless, you cannot immerse yourself in real life when you are constantly taking photos or keeping up with the likes on social media. Start by having family and friends make a' no dinner phone' rule. During an event, you can also take some pictures, but not at the risk of losing out on the action. Reflect more on living in the moment and having fun. Put your phone in the car or put it in silence and forget about it for a while, if you can't escape the lure. Social media is a great way to get in touch. On your feed, it can be easy to get lost for hours, from fellow peers to bosses and enjoyable with friends and family. The social media becomes an issue when it continuously takes you away from work and life. Perhaps these suggestions will help you to take control of your social media addiction.

4.3 Manage Your Attention, Not Your Time

With so many stimuli vying for attention and hope to make it throughout the day without our brains feeling like scrambled eggs are focused on being more mindful of how you care for specific tasks.

Here are three ways you can keep the energy going.

If there is anyone' guide' to efficacy, concentration is.

Philosopher of management, "At the end of the day my brain feels like the scrambled eggs! "Phil, an attorney to whose firm I teach, agreed. Like many, he was living out the consequences of what it means not to give workday focus. How do you find the energy to get something done when distractions abound?

Consider Awareness a Priority My previous post discussed what awareness is and why the quality of life, as well as significant effectiveness, are significant. Attention is a critical resource or resources that you need to invest in your experience. You're what you're attending to. That is so plain. Let's go for a moment on "Big Picture." Managing publicity wasn't on our radar screens, because most of us took it for granted until recently. Training has overwhelmingly stressed the ability to think and has under-emphasized, or completely ignored, the ability to participate, see, and interpret (let alone feel). Look at what is cut from school budgets when times are tough: arts, athletics, and music are the areas that promote awareness, concentration, and successful relationships. For good or for ill, we are a society of "I think so I am." Given that, it's easy to see how the focus can be missed even by the so-called "well trained."

Management expert Peter F. Drucker acknowledged that truly educated (and effective) people "will need fully trained vision as much as analytics" go forward. In a rapidly changing world, effective people will need to see as clearly as they think. It begins with controlling attention and focus. So many stimuli compete for attention, every hope for success depends on being more mindful of how you use it alone and with others.

The series of posts aims to create the points of discussion for you to have a conversation with those with whom you work and live to prioritize focus. The more you do so, the more you will be able to remain true to your goals, do your best, and involve the world in meaningful ways. So many stimuli compete for attention, every hope for efficacy depends on being more mindful of how you use it alone and with others.

Manage Focus Not Time. People tend to think that time management forms the basis for capable practice. Even Drucker said, "Time is the scarcest and most valuable resource of an executive," but I think that is a misperception. Who can handle the time, actually? Could you make the future easier, or come back to the past? If you aren't a sci-fi hero, no. All people do is control attention in the flow of time. Phil might block several hours to work on a case, for example, but if he spends those hours obsessing about baseball stats, we're saying he's mismanaged his time. His focus wasn't where it should have been. No-one is running time. We're paying attention. This point may sound like nit-picking, but I think it's important as it gives you a trigger that you can pull. What follows are real-life approaches my students and clients have built that worked for them.

Name Your Priorities It sounds simple, but I have found that we don't often enough name them. All too often, we allow the influence of anything that we've done to make our choices for us. Habits are perfect if they serve our true intentions or the real needs of a case. Otherwise, though we skip the important things, we wake up and go through the motions.

So, understanding what your goals are is the first and most essential step. Ask yourself: "What is important right now for me to put energy on? "And" Is this my best energy use? "These questions will help to clarify what's relevant. Intentions also help to tell the smaller (but perhaps more urgent) "no." Clarifying goals adds more clarity to energy investment. Habits are perfect if they serve our true intentions or the real needs of a case. Otherwise, when we skip the important things, we wake up and go through the motions. To explain your goals, ask yourself these questions: What are you doing to organize your day when you are constantly disrupted, and establish an action plan? To what's all right to say "no"? How do you cope with interruptions as they come up? Would you think you will respond to any interruptions? Were you worried that you'll be disliked/unloved/fired if you don't answer an email immediately? I have always found that people have much more freedom to say no to incoming requests, or "later," than they know. The short-and long-term goals include both. Now, that means choosing where to focus attention right now. Full this memo due tomorrow or look-up that you can't quite remember Yoda quote? In the long run, a sense of meaning and purpose is fundamental to where we put our focus. Is the diversion of Phil into baseball numbers, and not writing law briefs, an indication that he may be bored with being a lawyer? Is there anything else that he would rather do? In the long run, a sense of meaning and purpose is fundamental to where we put our focus.

Carry out an Attention Review to Increase Focus Understanding where attention should go will not help if you are unable to stay there. Focused attention removes distractions.

While I am not persuaded that it is possible to remove them entirely, great strides can be made in creating an environment that encourages and preserves publicity.

Look at your world, and what's there to help or hinder your attention. Frustrated marketing executive Evelyn stared through the prism of publicity at her office. She immediately noticed the copy machine for the office was put outside her house. Connected lines. She became annoyed, as her well-intentioned colleagues would stick their head in her door and talk while waiting for their copies. It happened several times an hour, and she never could find focused wind. Then Eureka! A phone call to the moving machine facility, and she eventually spent a day of rewarding concentration. Look around, and what are you going to do right now? Would you work in an environment open to the offices? What kind of signals would you give, saying, "Don't bother me? "These steps are but the start. One can build on and expand on each of these techniques. Note, be careful with yourself when starting this process. It takes time to develop and practice these critical skills to find the techniques that will help each one of us remain successful in turbulent times.

Chapter 5: Habits Switcher for Businessmen

Creating and Cultivating professional network. Introduction Managing your career can feel like a video game these days. It's easy to spend a whole day networking, from answering emails to handling documents to ticking off social media commitments–without even interacting with them. But while the increase of digital media has altered the landscape of networking, real professional relationships are just as important as ever. None will suggest an avatar for a task or sit down with a screen name for coffee to discuss opportunities. You need to focus more on developing a professional network somewhere along with the line-in person. But while the concept of a professional network is available to just about everyone, few put in the effort to create one. Here's what you can opt to start the process now, create a network that exists beyond an email thread or social network, and make it meaningful.

5.1 Find a Mentor

Having someone you really like and admire is the first step in finding a mentor. That may sound like a zero-brainer but how often people let that aspect fall to the side of the road is shocking. Prospective mentees can let the charisma, reputation, or skill of an individual lure them into what could be a disastrous partnership for both parties–don't do that. The mentor-mental relationship rule should be the same as any other. Both parties should like each other, value each other, and appreciate each other's enterprise in general. Anything else will certainly not encourage a fruitful long-term relationship.

Once you have met someone you admire and want to connect with, go ahead with caution. Too many people are getting an invitation to "choose their brain" over coffee. While some people may say "yes" to this question, you may also get negative (or none) responses from people who are simply too busy.

Deal a mutually beneficial deal. "Instead of asking them if you can just' pick their brain,' give something in exchange, like helping them study a project or perhaps collaborating with them through an apprenticeship," says freelance writer Jackie Lam of Chapters.

I still believe you can use an apprenticeship to establish new connections that offer a job or have your mentor suggest you for a job.

Connect on social media; Social media has made networking a possibility with your dream mentors. He recommends that you use LinkedIn and other sites to develop a relationship with them. But this does not mean adding them immediately as a link and submitting a list of your most burning questions. Creating a professional relationship like a romantic one takes time. "Sharing and commenting on their posts/tweets over time, answering questions they ask, and building a relationship, "says Schneider. "Engage them with industry and job questions after this has been developed." Experts recommend having an established group tailored for people in your area. You can come across like-minded people who can share their own advice. One place to do this is on the Meetup local get-together platform, which for every sector has a lot of professional networking groups. Link in the real world Become a member of one of these networks, and you will first learn about opportunities or possibilities. You might even find people to personally suggest you–a huge advantage in an era where you can find every job posting online.

"Proven thing you can do for long-term career success, whether you're just graduating or already beginning your career, is to build a network of supporters," says Huffman. Maximize Your Personal Network Carla LaFleur, who serves as a media and public relations consultant for Halpern

Financial, a wealth-management firm, says you can find people you already meet who might have a link to the sector you want to enter into.

"I asked my uncle, who's a CPA for advice on how to get into the world of fee-only financial planning, for instance. He directed me to study the trade unions, and some red flags to stop, "she says. Family and friends. Make a list of people you know that may have experience of the work or area that you want to try. Also, you can ask your family or close friends who might have a connection and be happy to set up you. It can help you sit down with a notebook and list every person you meet–and then personally reach out to them. And don't think about your alma mater. If you have graduated recently, you should also reach out to your alma mater's career services department. They should be able to give feedback on any alumni who are also involved in the area. You may also be familiar with internships or employment within that sector. Perhaps your mentor in high school can know what their past students are up to, and how they can help.

5.2 Reach Former Colleagues

Old bosses and colleagues, even if you're trying to switch jobs, are great people to touch too. You've already done a lot of work to communicate with them, and you'll get a better idea of what they can give you. Work with groups in the city. Huffman recommends joining a party that isn't relevant to your business either. You may, for example, volunteer for an agency you care about or join your college's alumni association, which may have frequent networking events. "It gives you more opportunities to volunteer your charity skills for the resume and will serve as a platform for others who may be looking for that ability in their work," he said. "Also, many prominent individuals from large corporations serve on the boards of most charities."

Meet New People Usually; an old-fashioned phone call will be preferable to any type of digital communication when you want to start a conversation with someone new. A telephone call is more intimate, more straightforward, and more likely to give you an answer. If you feel nervous about calling someone cold, you can also send an initial email and only call if you do not get a response. Come prepared with questions. Come prepared. If you have already undertaken basic research, you should have a list of questions ready for your mentor or future touch. Not having done the groundwork shows you don't value the time or energy of this individual and is an easy way to brighten a bridge. Even the third party who set up the meeting could damage your relationship. Listen rather than you're talking. Don't act like a salesman for a used car. While using this meeting to sell your experience and qualifications might be tempting, LaFleur's advice is to listen more than you speak.

"In my experience, being a good listener makes a better impression and asking smart questions rather than trying to pitch the get-go skills out of it," she said. "The purpose of this first discussion is simply to learn and meet new people, but do it as many times as possible, and you are likely to get some opportunities," she asks. "And" What are the ingredients that make someone successful in this field? "Treat it like an interview. Treat the meeting as an interview for a job. Although this contact might not result in work, you still should treat it as such.

That means you might suggest that you dress professionally and behave like this person for a role. You don't need to wear a suit so leave home the jeans. Show curiosity. Get something to know about them.

Whether you find out that they're an inexperienced water skier or are constantly posting pictures of their new puppy on Instagram, it's important to show interest in something outside of your career. It will give off the feeling that you really want to get to know them–instead of just exploiting their professional status for personal growth.

Experts say, "The best networking doesn't feel like networking; it feels like having a conversation with a trusted friend or colleague." That doesn't mean you've got to make this person your best new friend but communicating in an honest and personal manner is important. If the touch with which you are networking is a little reluctant, think about opening at your end. Don't gush about yourself, but it's not just a one-way street to give them friendship. Please do not forget to say thank you. Send a note of thanks. Whether you're meeting at your local Starbucks or getting a virtual meeting via Skype, don't forget to send physical anything. Sure, a hand-written old-fashioned, thank you for a message. Sending a thank-you note will help you stand apart from other applicants or individuals who are vying for their time. You can even paste a small gift card in a coffee shop as an extra thank-you if you really want to please anyone. I acknowledged and sent a thank-you note that same day after I had an in-person interview for a job I truly wanted. Earlier my boss said that it helped him determine that I was the right candidate. Stay in touch. It is also critical that you stay in touch. People are busy, so if you have just one meeting and don't stay connected (beyond an initial thank-you note), they'll probably forget about you when an opportunity arises. Don't be afraid to touch base frequently on what you were up to. On the other end of the spectrum, they are to be congratulated at personal achievements and demonstrate an appreciation of the highlights of their careers. LinkedIn is great for finding out what's new in their work-life, and it's easy to send a quick note of congratulations.

5.3 Build a Customer Centric Culture in Your Organization

Each organization or company exists at its heart to fulfil certain needs, to solve certain problems, and to meet certain demands. There's no point in running your business if there are no buyers for what your company is making or selling. And, in fact, it's your customers who run the show, make you money and pay your employees ' salaries. In return, they reasonably expect you to care about their issues, work hard to create goods that make their lives comfortable and easier, and stay alert in solving any bottlenecks in their path to success. That is all about customer-centricity. A customer-centric organization is where each process begins and ends with a view of customer satisfaction. It is not an event but a culture — an ideology, and not an isolated action. I've outlined some important facts and figures in one of my previous posts on how customer frustration can lead to huge monetary losses and long-term costs. A customer-centric culture has the opposite effect altogether. It lends direction to your employees ' efforts and ultimately leads to increased customer retention and monetary gains. Here's how you can create and reap the benefits of a customer-centric culture within your organization.

Make customer satisfaction a central part of your customer values. Even before you start practicing it, customer-centricity should be a part of the philosophy of your company. This may be sounding like a formality, but it has a profound impact on the business strategy of your company, its attitude towards customer issues, and how customer satisfaction is perceived by its employees. Articulate your customer-first philosophy concisely. Micah Solomon, a customer-related expert at Forbes, recommends elaborating this philosophy in a clear and easy-to-understand list of core values that your company intends to uphold. It needs to address your values to both internal and external clients, your values against your customers, staff, and vendors. This is the groundwork required to lay the foundations of a strong customer-centric culture in your company. A reliable email management system is a crucial part of customer-centric machinery. You'll be handling customer communications with absolute ease with Hiver's Shared Inbox. I want to know more.

Creating awareness in your organization Customer-Centric Culture-Customer Centricity awareness isn't just a buzzword. It's an attitude towards doing business that can produce monetary gains over the long term and raise the brand value. It has tangible effects and can be calculated over time. According to Forrester's Customer Experience Index 200 (CEI 200), compared to their competitors, businesses with a customer-cantered community have a higher value. And further figures back up that claim. The odds of selling to a customer who is already on board, for example, is 50-70%. It is just 5-20 percent for new prospects. You need to create awareness about it using facts like these to establish a customer-centric culture in your business. Customer-centricity can't be achieved unless most of your organization truly believes in its impact and benefits. Market the effect of customer satisfaction on company performance actively and ensure that your staff and anyone related to your organization knows that customer satisfaction is at the heart of your business values. You are using posters, images, banners, and other signs to disseminate the core customer-centric principles throughout the organization. You also need to ensure all your staff have access to the customer input you received. In short, make it clear to anyone who enters your business that customer satisfaction tops your priority list.

Put customer satisfaction ahead of everything else. If you put your customers ahead of everything else, you are, in fact choosing the most important stakeholder in your company. Because as I said earlier, customers are paying your wages and bringing you profits. Even if it means cancelling important meetings, revising timetables, losing holidays, and sometimes giving up money, each person in your organization should understand the importance of your customers and be assured that they will be rewarded for sacrificing certain tasks to ensure their satisfaction, in keeping with your core values. This also means you need to motivate your employees to make - the-spot decisions for your customers and give them the right authority and trust. Give their clients control and encourage them to make rational decisions where possible. Verify that you provide them with the best tools to do their jobs. For example, most companies have an email account to manage their customer questions and concerns, such as support@xyz.com. It will be mentioned often on the company's website, making it one of the easiest ways for customers to get their voices heard. You should use Hiver to handle these email accounts if you want to create a truly customer-centric organization. The delegation, monitoring, and automation features can help make it easier to effectively manage and respond to customer tickets.

Reward Employees for Customer Satisfaction, each aspect of your business, should be associated with the sole purpose of creating an optimal customer experience to become a customer-centric organization. You need a motivated team that sees personal gains in customer satisfaction for this to materialize. Intelligent companies do this by combining employee growth and customer satisfaction opportunities. They reward employees who go the extra mile to solve customer problems or create something that makes end-users ' lives easier. While a relatively new concept in measuring customer satisfaction, there are a few methods that will help you measure it. That way, it can still be a part of your performance management process for your employees. For example, last year, I worked with a web-based start-up (which had grown to nearly 300 employees), which directly linked the growth of its management layer employees with growth figures for the business and customer feedback. If workers have a personal stake in customer satisfaction, their method of thinking shifts entirely. This establishes a corporate culture in which everyone aims to satisfy the consumer and where top performers are not only decided based on sales figures.

Get Everyone Involved with Customer-Centric Culture-Team-Building You can't just focus on your customer service department when you want to build a customer-centric culture within your company. Everybody wants to get involved and really consider what the consumers want. It includes the product development and engineering teams, the divisions for sales and services, and the key decision-makers for your business. For example, Groove's CEO Alex Turnbull spends 20 + hours per week serving customers. He sits with the support teams instead of hiding behind his glass office and stays in direct contact with the customers. Other innovative companies regularly ask their engineering teams to spend a few hours doing customer support or receiving direct feedback from the customers. Some of them find unhappy customers and get them on a conference call with all the company's key decision-makers. If the middle-and lower-level employees see your company's top management playing an active role in customer satisfaction, they will also start to value it.

The process of creating a customer-centric culture in your company starts with hiring the right staff and creating the right standards. Every professional entering the company should understand the value that customer satisfaction puts on you. They need to be ready to go the extra mile for your customers and understand that there is a stake in every employee in your business. Customer cantering is a core value of your market. All your staff should be in alignment with that. It will also serve as a guide in your hiring and firing decisions. You're well off without people who don't believe in your core values. And the consumer centricity results aren't stopping only there. The goods you produce and the solutions you provide should represent that. The resources you employ from third parties or any smaller companies that you buy should be in accordance with your principles. Facebook's purchases on Instagram or WhatsApp are great examples of that.

Celebrate Customer Success Centre Culture-Celebrate Success Unlike conventional organizations, the relationship between customer-centric companies and their customers does not only associate with the provision of service/products. We are equally concerned with the actual value we provide the consumers. They celebrate the success of their customers and lend a helping hand when it is difficult for the customer to obtain full-service value. If a customer derives extra value from your programs, then use it to inspire your staff as a success story. Consider it an experience, reward, and thank the people involved in providing value to that customer for their hard work. For example, when a TradeKey.com service employee, a B2B trading platform, was able to help a customer successfully complete a huge business transaction, the entire team involved in providing value to that customer (including the technical and administrative teams) were praised and honoured for their efforts. Try creating a community in your business where everything is celebrated as activities, from customer acquisition and on boarding to retention and renewal. Wrapping it up: a proactive approach is required to develop a customer-centric culture. Customer centricity is often seen as a subjective topic that cannot be clearly defined and tracked. But it does have well-documented long-term monetary and branding advantages. Starting with your corporate values, you need to create an environment where every employee in your company considers customer satisfaction before making any decisions. In making this part of your employee compensation and reward system, and by giving an example to your higher management staff, you will be on your way to creating a genuinely customer-centric company.

5.4 Humbleness

Humbly recognizing our shortcomings, having faith in Christ, and repenting, He will make things bad strong. We can be filled with peace when we seek the truth and realize that the truth is what makes us free. Humility the Saviour proclaimed, "I offer humility unto men, that they may be humble; and my grace is sufficient unto all men that humble themselves before me; for if individuals will humble themselves and have firm believe in me, then will I make them strong to weak things" (Ether 12:27). As we transform in humility towards God, He will motivate us to conquer our sins. Pride leads us to hide and fail, but modesty leads us to be accessible, teachable, and eager to seek assistance. Honesty Being honest will allow us to transform successfully on our journey. We can start by looking at our lives and our progress. The efforts will be more successful as we also understand the potential consequences of the actions— both positive and negative. To embrace the truth about our lives allows us to accept information and insights that might inspire our efforts to change. If we have an inaccurate picture of our unhealthy behaviour, however, we could be cutting ourselves off from personal revelation and support from others. Denial, deflection, minimization, rationalization, denying, accusing, and deception are all ways of delusion— first of ourselves, then of others.

Honesty brings peace, which makes our lives easier. Honest living begins with a determination to put an end to patterns of hiding, living double lives, deceiving our loved ones, and putting up a facade of being ok when we are not. Recognizing our need for help combating pornography allows us to get help from appropriate sources. We can begin to regain the trust of our loved ones, as we do our best, to be honest. Moreover, being honest and humble opens our hearts to seek help from our Father in Heaven and the Saviour and prepares us to discover insights and follow the Spirit's prompts to repent and heal. Experts stated: "Humility and honesty are critical. If you are to cease to be a natural man and become a saint through the expiation of Christ the Lord, it is important to become' as a child, submissive, meek, modest, patient, full of love, willing to submit to all that the Lord sees fit to inflict on him' (Mosiah 3:19). "Humility and sincerity seeking the truth lead us to seek the truth and enable us to dispel darkness.

As we learn how to transcend the use of pornography from reliable sources, we can feel hope and restore peace to our lives. We, too, can be free from the opponent's lies. Studying Jesus Christ's mission and His atoning sacrifice will build our trust and faith in Him. As we grow in our Saviour's love and understanding, we can move along the path to joyful repentance. Repentance is a blessing common to us all as we humble ourselves before Him. Capture Impressions Take a moment to write down what you felt while you were researching this theory. Apply This Principle The following are some helps to improve the understanding and implementation of this principle on additional subjects. It was one slip. Do I have to tell them? It's important for others to be humble and honest. Most of us are slipping up as we try to change our habits and behaviours. Transition is a phase and will not occur immediately. Being frank about our relapses helps us to keep moving forward. Secrecy leads us to guilt, which makes returning to pornography easier for us. Why does that continue to happen? Be humble to yourself and be honest. Lasting change comes when we are frank with ourselves and when we have soft hearts. The Saviour will help us conquer them because we realize our shortcomings.

5.5 Ask for help from Experts

I get it — there are some people out there who would rather walk nude into work than sucking up their pride and asking for assistance. For some purposes, a request for assistance is interpreted by many of us as a sign of weakness when, in fact, I think it is a sign of great power. Yeah, that means you are sufficiently self-aware and self-assured to know when it is time to call in some reinforcements. But that doesn't automatically mean it's easy to request help. Nope, it can be quite anxiety-inducing to approach someone in your office to ask him or her to lend a hand. So, here are four times when it's undoubtedly time to bite the bullet and ask — along with a recommendation on what to say in each case. Because the very last thing you want to do is gather your strength just to stammer your way through a vague and rambling submission.

If you do not have an idea of what you are doing, OK, then this one should be obvious. But if you have no idea what you are supposed to do for a work project, it is time for some clarification and assistance to approach someone in your office. There's no use torturing your mind by trying to navigate blindly through a challenging project you don't understand. If you do that, odds are it won't turn out as expected, and you're going to have wasted your own time (and everybody else!). Plus, you're going to look stubborn and incompetent. So, calm down, sit and take a deep breath and approach your boss or one of your co-workers to get a better understanding of the specific task and objectives. Try this: "Hey, I'm feeling somewhat confused about XYZ project details.

Can we set a time for sitting down, going through this assignment's nuts and bolts and make sure we're on the same page? When your mind is overburden, the best of us happens.

You kept answering with enthusiasm: "Absolutely! "You're completely buried under work for every idea that landed in your lap. You have hit your mark, and you know there's just no way you're going to finish it all by the deadline even if you've been pulling all-nights for the next three weeks. What is your next move? Request some help from your other teammates.

You may feel as though you are shirking responsibility. But, in this situation, everyone has been in his or her life at least once. The next time your colleague feels overwhelmed, just be sure to pay back the favour! Try this: "I don't like feeling like I'm trying to pass off other people's work, but right now, I'm completely swamped. Do you mind helping me with the XYZ part of this project if you have any extra time? I know this is your expertise, and I would really like your advice and guidance! "Four. You are human when you make a mistake, and mistakes are almost inevitable. Yet, it's not exactly what you've done; it's about how you've reacted to it. The last and worst thing you can do is try to sweep it under the rug without acknowledging anyone. And, if you try to remedy your mistake by engaging in areas or departments where you don't really belong, you might well make your problem even worse. Which is humiliating. However, if you need help fixing your slip-up, be sure to immediately approach the appropriate people in your office. It's not like that you are the only person who makes a mistake at work — and obviously, you're not the last one. Try this: "I'm so sorry, but I've totally messed up with ABC, and now I need XYZ to fix it. I'm so sorry for the overwork and frustration. I appreciate your help! "Five. If you need extra skills or guidance, even if you're an utter freak of nature, you already know that your priority should be on finding the best possible job— not just something that has your name all over it.

So, if you're working on a project that you think will benefit greatly from your co-workers' additional input, never hesitate to ask them to provide their guidance and talents. It encourages teamwork among your team members and helps to make the best it can be for your project. Speak a win-win. Try this: "I am working on the XYZ project and I'd love your input from the expert in this specific area. Can we set up a meeting when we can speak with each other and bounce off their ideas? In fact, I think your feedback can carry this project to the next stage! "Asking for help isn't always easy. Yet, sometimes it's essential. When you think that you are in one of these scenarios, take a deep breath, swallow your pride and, for some much-needed help, ask others in your workplace. I promise — in the long term, it'll be great for you.

Chapter 6: Habits Switcher for Kids

Habits Switcher are the qualities that still lack in our kids, despite of whatever age they have. If you have trouble figuring out how to enrich their personality with Few good habits, how to keep your mind away from pessimist approach or unhealthy habits, how to indulge your personality in positive habits through various exercises, tactics, what are the benefits of Habits Switcher and what is the skillset of a person who is adaptive to Habits Switcher? This chapter has covered all the untapped area for kids and much more

6.1 Opting Physical Activities & Healthy Diet

Choosing Physical Exercise & Healthy Diet Healthy Eating Children tend mostly to demand quick snacks, cookies, candy, biscuits, and chocolates. You must make them think that even healthy food will taste as good as that. A homemade version of noodles, pasta, pies, cookies, and pizza can be served to them too. To make kids build this healthy habit, go the fun route –make it an aim to consume each rainbow colour once a week, which means eating foods in a meal of different colours. Not only does it have mind and health benefits, but it also makes sure the kids have fun eating. Parents are the ones to whom kids will follow, so they should set a healthy example by eating regular, nutritious, and well-balanced foods.

Physical activity It would be a huge mistake on your part as a parent to encourage your kids to sit and get cozy on the couch and watch TV. Don't let your children find themselves in a sedentary lifestyle. Encourage them to make them go, perhaps for a walk or workout, or send them out for outdoor play. Plan a family activity, make it fun, and involve your kids. Inform the children that being a couch potato has adverse health effects.

Some of the unhealthy a sedentary lifestyle poses are as follows: Focus on Food-Nutrition Labels, Not Designer Ones At a certain age, especially around their teenage years, your children get interested in their clothing labels. Continue to educate your kids about the more relevant labels they will note from young age-food labels. Once they get into the habit, they allow them to think in the same way about the nutritional value of the food. Show them their favourite packaged foods and point out the essential nutrition label information. Consider it their practice to read those labels, evaluate the nutritional value, and then determine their value. Have them focus on key ingredients like saturated and unsaturated fats, sugar, calories and carbs? Your conscious endeavours will help develop healthy habits they will carry throughout their lives.

Enjoy Family Meals Together There's hardly any quality time left to spend with family and elders in the hectic life that we live in today. A busy working life could end up meaning you can't sit with kids and listen to their stories and personal questions. Make it a priority to spend dinner time with all members of your family. You should discuss several things and share your views with each other; this will affect the children for a long time. Few other pros of eating together include the following: Children begin to get comfortable and adjust well within the family Children develop good eating habits and avoid junk food when they get stronger Healthy Hydration Pro Tip with elders: Drink water, not soft drinks. Drinking unhealthy drinks is the most common trait adopted by the elderly emulating little ones. You must direct your kids, reinforce the value of drinking water, and avoid soda.

Only tell the children that water is safe and helps to get rid of several diseases, while soft drinks are bad because they have a lot of sugar content and add calories, causing weight problems.

Educate them that intake of water is necessary and is a vital resource and that enough quantities should be taken to maintain proper hydration. Once your children know how important water is for their bodies, they are sure to choose it over aerated unhealthy drinks.

Set up a routine to spend some time together for a physical activity like walking, jogging, swimming, running, or doing yoga at home. Over the long term, exercise will prove beneficial to the whole family. Starting it in the kid's routine early will keep them healthy, comfortable, and flexible. It'll help set your kids a healthy lifestyle. Putting on music will bring some spice to your workout. The optimal approach to do this is to have your child participate in some sport. It will teach them valuable lessons in life too, the most important being that of sportsmanship. Engaging in regular physical activity, Dedicate 40 minutes to everyday physical activity.

Kids should be kept physically active by involving them in interesting activities, whether they are playing sports, musical instruments, swimming, or gymnastics. The habit will improve your children's development in all ways. Children will remain healthy and alert; they will learn to be strong, and in later adulthood, they are likely to continue those activities. If your kids aren't fond of sports or dread going to gym class, continue to encourage them to try new things and introduce them to other events. Sooner or later, they'll find something certainly challenging, pleasurable and enjoyable.

Cleanliness must be taught to kids early on in life by design. Start by arranging things around kids properly. We will want to keep it that way too when they get used to seeing things in an orderly fashion.

Once they are old enough, you can encourage them and delegate time to clean up the mess. By doing so often, they will soon learn and try to organize their own things themselves.

Be Responsible with Money You can start educating them about the value of your hard-earned money as soon as your children are a teenager and responsible enough to use the money to go and buy things. You can get your kids into the habit of saving money occasionally, giving them pocket money, or keep a savings account for them. Give them a budget and promote spending and saving money. Your kids will learn the value of the money and start saving this way. Sharing is caring Children should be aware of the value of certain things, learn to be thankful and be gracious enough to share with those who cannot afford them. Teach them the intangible things which can also be conveyed, such as emotions, worries, and stories. Next, children will learn to share with their families— parents, grandparents, siblings, relatives, extended families, and then others. The exchange of mentality would make him or her a better person.

Don't Litter Public Spaces Elevate your children to culture and responsible citizenship. Explain that public spaces and parks are not intended for littering, and that waste should be put into the nearest dustbin. Help them to develop this basic habit and encourage them to practice it everywhere, as it will help them to grow into better individuals. Make it a habit of not littering, and your children will follow your example with certainty. When outside the house, still look for dustbins to throw things away. When you step out of the house and collect all your waste in it, you can carry a small plastic bag with you-empty water bottles, paper napkins, etc. Bring it home and place it in the dustbin instead of just leaving it at the restaurant's table or tossing it on the side of the road, or out the window of the car.

6.2 Be Courteous & Unbiased

Be courteous is a virtue that is admired by all. Teach your children how to respect people, either they are elder or younger than them. Teach them that they should be polite and part ways in a decent manner even if they encounter individuals they don't like very much. They ought to be calm and cordial to all. Throughout their lives, those qualities will remain with them, and they will always be looked upon with respect. First, treat your children with respect, and you're going to see that they're going to grab on that habit on their own. Be courteous towards the purifier. Kids do see kids do. Be Unbiased Children are born innocent and unbiased, and that distinction is part of social conditioning. As a parent, you just need to keep your kids away from the tendency to discriminate. Teach them to be unbiased and treat everyone equally, whether rich or poor, friend or foe. You should allow them to be friends of every faith or caste with children.

Do not harm animals or birds. Children are usually excited about birds and animals. Many feels attracted, some are afraid of them, some become aggressive, some remain calm. They should be educated that animals and birds are living creatures who communicate and can be friendly in their own ways. We should learn to distinguish between dangerous creatures and no harmful ones.

Please advise them to stay away from harmful ones and be friendly and kind to pets. Through televising them with documentaries and animal shows, you will teach them about the same. Do Not Criticize or Bully Someone Rather constructively point out mistakes and shortcomings. Criticism can make children or kill them. Not everybody is wise enough to take positive critical comments at a young age. Parents need to watch and guide their children closely regarding their interaction and mannerisms.

It should be made kids realize that criticism will affect others, so they shouldn't speak ill of others. Unnecessary teasing or bullying someone you hardly know is wrong and not acceptable just for the sake of fun. A point to ponder for parents is to never speak ill of members of your family before your child.

Be honest: Do not lie to your kids. Even lies that are white are lies. Try and always be as honest as possible. Honesty is a very necessary virtue and must be practiced in children from infancy onwards. Being a parent, you are your children's role model. They have the greatest impact on your actions and words, optimistic as well as negative. Be frank always, especially with children in attendance. In every circumstance, motivate them to speak the truth. Patience and perseverance Encourage them to take up gardening or cook. Patience is a virtue' is rightly said, because patients can be at ease, and peace is what everyone in today's chaotic world is seeking. Inculcate the children's tolerance early so that they grow up happy and peaceful. Teach them to relax, remain calm, and wait at their own pace for their turn or for certain events to occur. Assure them that diligence certainly pays off, and any adverse situations can be treated with ease. Encourage and support them to participate in activities such as gardening or cooking where results are not instantaneous, and patience is needed.

Pay Gratitude Grow the habit of praying twice a day. Promote a humble attitude in your family, and encourage them to be thankful for everything, big and small. Cultivate the practice of praying twice a day, waking up in the morning and bedtime before going to bed. Do it on your own, and your kids will benefit from you. Help Others Encourage kids to help one person daily.

Raise your children to be of a helpful nature. Display them modesty and kindness along the way. Encourage them to give those in need a helping hand whenever and wherever possible. Do your part; help people in the presence of your children, whether it's a friend or a stranger, but at the same time warn them to be careful around strangers.

6.3 Stay Clean & Hygienic

Wash Hands Tell them about germs and illnesses they can pick up because of unclean hands. The most popular etiquette taught to kindergarten students is washing one's hands before and after meals. Let them know that handwashing can prevent common illnesses like flu, cold, and other infections. You need to teach them the mandatory basic rules for healthy life: Wash your hands before and after meals or after playing in sand Use clean dry towels, or perhaps tissues, to dry hands Use antibacterial hand washes Brushing Twice A Day Do it together–brush your teeth along with your infant. Oral hygiene is very critical and includes early childhood treatment. The habits that were imparted early on will remain for a long time. Children often become lazy about brushing their teeth, but this routine task should not be taken lightly. On occasion, you can treat them with their favorite sweets as a reward. Brush them daily and twice daily Gargle post meals- This helps to avoid bad breath, and cavities Floss the teeth at appropriate times Clean the tongue with a tongue cleaner Don't share your toothbrush Clean Ears Do it as part of drying up after a bath.

Ears are some of the body's most vital organs. Neglecting your ears clean may result in a lot of discomfort and even infections. One must be very vigilant to periodically clean the ears, starting from infancy.

The outer ear should be water-cleaned and washed with a dry towel every day as kids grow up; you can teach them how to clean their own ears. Daily Showers Shower in summertime twice a day. Showering is a fundamental necessity that is recommended for people of all ages. After waking up, it must be done the first thing in the morning. During the hot summer days, you can have your kids shower twice. Instead, after playing outdoors, your kids should take a shower when they come home. Showering nourishes the skin and makes them feel fresh, ready for the day and sleep a good night.

Keep the hair clean Teach children how to comb their hair properly. Children need to keep their hair clean. Often the scalp and hair get dirty when driving or playing outdoors. They should wash their hair frequently, as little as once in two or three days. This will keep them safe from an infestation of the lice, dandruff, and excessive hair fall. Make it a habit to regularly apply oil to their scalp before they wash. Make sure you also use a comb that also brushes the scalp while combing their hair. This improves scalp blood circulation and promotes healthy hair growth.

Keeping Nails Short Explain to them how their nails can cause germs to enter the body, Babies often tend to place their fingers in their mouth, so keeping the nails clean and free from dirt is necessary. As kids grow up, you can coach them about the need to keep their nails short and clean. How their nails can allow germs to enter the body by scratching or through the mouth can be explained to them, thereby making them ill. You need to start teaching them about the value of good health and good habits as your children grow older enough to enter school. Apart from the healthy habits mentioned above, here are some important ones that school kids can follow: No Smoking, Drinking, and Drugs Stop these habits yourself, and your child will follow suit.

Habits like alcohol, smoking, and drugs depend largely on the history and upbringing of the family. Ensure that you are fully involved in the lives of your children, knowing their shortcomings and helping them always when neglect and lack of communication leave them vulnerable to outside influences. You need to educate your children about such unhealthy habits and, in all cases, teach them to keep away. Always warn the children not to come under peer control. As a dad, you can benefit from not getting yourself drunk and smoking first. You may be teaching discipline to your children, but whether or not your child implements it will depend on how well you, as a parent, inculcate it in everyday life. Show them the right path and encourage them, with positive reinforcement and praise, to remain on it.

6.4 Having A Healthy and Positive Mind-Set

"Yes," "Thank You," and "Sorry" Use these terms as often as you can, with your children and before them. The four magical words, "Please," "Thank you", "Humbled" and "Sorry" should be taught to your children, which will help them tackle many problems with ease. The habit of using those golden words always makes one in a society known and revered. Your kids come across as polite, warm-hearted people. Practice these words with your children regularly, and then they will also use those greetings. Children are susceptible and quickly get discouraged by little things or when things don't go their way or the way they have planned.

It is key point that you get involved and talk to them, so you know what your kids are going through and what they're talking about, so they don't get into any negative self-talk. Avoid false praise; instead, ensure that their achievements and efforts are acknowledged on time.

By giving them confidence on their capabilities and unique qualities and stressing that they are loved no matter what, you can help children develop self-esteem. Try to develop their outlook so that they can have a positive mindset and think positively when faced with challenging situations all through their lives.

Spend time with Friends planning weekends play-dates. It's said friendships formed in school stay longer, maybe even for a lifetime. This is because children have naive minds; they have no selfish motives to make friends. And at young age friends are playing a very important role in your children's social growth. By being with peers, children learn valuable life skills such as communication, socialization, coordination, problem-solving, and teamwork. Good friends become a part of your child support system through adolescence and adulthood. Encourage your kids to make friends and spend time with them socializing and relaxing.

Don't skip breakfast. Ensure that they get a healthy, nutritious start to the day. Breakfast is the main meal for all ages. It is especially important for children and school-going adolescents, as it kick-starts the functions of the brain, metabolism, and body and provides energy throughout the day. For their meal, you can provide your children with high-fiber cereals, as they help reduce the risk of diabetes and heart disease. Getting used to breakfast in their adulthood will prove beneficial for them. Let them know the harmful consequences that breakfast skipping has and emphasize that not eating in the morning increases the chances of obesity. Table Manners Start early and foster freedom. Children have insisted on having meals themselves after a certain age. Although they may like to carry spoons and forks, they struggle to do so properly and instead create a mess. They need to be trained to eat well on their own. You should handle them as grown-ups and start showing them the proper ways of getting meals.

Read Every Day Make it a part of the bedtime routine for your kids. The best way to inculcate your children's love for reading is to make it part of the playtime and bedtime routine for your children. Select books that would make your children read a treat. Consider it a daily habit and keep it, as it will help build the self-esteem of the children, improve their reading skills, and grow their imagination, vocabulary, and creativity. This appears to be helpful in strengthening parental relationships and communication. Quality Time Fosters timeliness. We know the phrase "time is money" and know both the value of time and money. Kids need to be trained to use the time properly, learn to get ready on time, obey daily schedules, and be on time. Make them understand the need to get to school on time because they might be disciplined for not being punctual. You can attend multiple functions or parties as a family. Make sure you aim for every moment before or on time, and they will inculcate the same patterns as the children grow.

Sleep on Time Set a standard routine for bedtime. Rest is important for both a growing baby and a young child. During your childhood, you need to instill the routine "Early to bed, late to rise" in your children early on. Every day, school-going children need to be busy and healthy, for which they require proper sleep. Sleep helps the body recover all the expended energy during the day. Late sleeping will help your kids get enough rest and make the kids feel fresh and healthy the next day.

Put your kids in early sleep, and sleep with them. Keeping you nearby will make your kids feel safe and have a healthy sleep Go to sleep early every day; this will help set the routine for the kids, and they will learn to sleep on their own Avoid letting your kids sleep on a stretch for more than the time required. If needed, the children may have a short nap through their failures during the afternoon Accept Defeat Support them.

Children are prone to feel annoyed when they fail. Parents will play critical role to help them and inspire them to take the loss positively, and next time give their best. They need to be informed of the ups and downs of life and made to understand that not all defeats are permanent. It's not always about winning or loses. It's also crucial the effort you put in and the progress you make. Work Hard Teach your kids that life is without shortcuts! Enlighten the children by the value of hard work. Cultivate the habit of putting everything they do into their best efforts, be it reading, writing, or any meaningful job. We will know that good luck alone does not favor success; it takes hard work and determination. You should give your children an example of how hard you're working to earn a living.

Chapter 7: Pessimist Mindset- Hurdle in Altering Habits Switcher

The traditional definition of pessimist thinking is, "to think too much or too long about something." While it is human nature to think things through when deciding or analysing a situation, it becomes pessimist thinking when you cannot get out of your own mind. At some point in our lives, it happens to all of us-we all encounter things that cause us to worry or stress. But it appears some people can't turn off their concerns. We are worried about the future, making disastrous predictions about unlikely events that have not yet occurred. We even ruminate about the past, bashing themselves about "would haves" and "should haves." They're concerned about what others might think of them or let their minds build up negative self-talk. Also, pessimist thinking a tough decision that you need to make can cause problems. Playing all the options in your head can lead to "analysis paralysis"-you're afraid to take the wrong action, so you don't take any action. But it is easier even to make the wrong decision than to make no decision. You've probably suffered sleepless nights where your brain just won't turn off, whether you're a chronic over thinker or have a tough decision to make. Pessimist thinking can enhance symptoms of depression, escalate stress levels and affect your judgement.

7.1 Pessimist Mindset

There is no such thing as pessimist thinking illness. There are many different types of anxiety disorders in which a person participates in pessimist thinking or ruminating, but no disorder exists.

When an individual cannot stop being obsessed and worried about things, it can affect your quality of life.

Several mental health diagnoses where a person can't stop his or her brain from ruminating include PTSD, depression, agoraphobia, panic disorder, selective mutism, separation anxiety disorder, social anxiety disorder, phobias, substance-induced anxiety disorder, or it could possibly be a symptom of some other disease. Many of these have pessimist thinking as a symptom when it comes to anxiety disorders. For example, when they are going to have a panic attack again, a person with a panic disorder might ruminate and overthink. They obsessed with something which could cause their assault. We are not only nervous, but now they have meta-anxiety, which is anxiety about being anxious. It felt more difficult to overthink their panic attack. Pessimist thinking is prevalent. You need not have an anxiety disorder in order to engage in excessive rumination. You might argue that's part of the human condition. At times, we all overthink things: You may be overly concerned about what you have said or done to someone. You may be preoccupied with performing at school or at work. You may be preoccupied with how others see you. Mentioned examples of how you could become interested in pessimist thinking.

Some forms of pessimist thinking include: — When you're concerned about what you should have said or done— performance anxiety, or worried about how you measure up to others at work— participating in "what - if" scenarios where you're wondering what might happen in a variety of circumstances— catastrophic or worst-case thinking — worrying about getting an unforeseen panic attack— excessive Most people are suffering from obsessions and fears about issues beyond their influence.

Cognitive Behaviour Therapy (CBT) is commonly used standard therapies for such anxiety. CBT helps people confront their negative or irrational beliefs and turn their emotions into constructive, productive ones.

Having anxiety therapy or medication can make a huge difference for a pessimist thinking person. You can contact a therapist in your city and can have a detailed discussion with him/her, or with one of certified mental health professionals here. Virtual therapy is an ideal place to work on anxiety and to start learning to develop coping skills.

Pessimist thinking Most people are familiar with the term anxiety disorder (and in fact, millions of people suffer every day from some type of anxiety disorder), but we tend to overlook a major anxiety disorder symptom that overthinks.

The definition of pessimist thinking is anything to ruminate or obsess. A lot of people may think they are over thinkers after hearing this description. Who doesn't go a single day without trying to overthink something? We are certain if we are making the correct or impactful choices from small things like picking the fastest route that morning on our commute or choosing the right restaurant for dinner to things like the well-being of our children and the safety and security of our family. But it is normal. To some extent, it is normal in stress and overthinks. Nevertheless, pessimist thinking can have harmful effects on a person mentally and emotionally. It would be monotonous thoughts about something that causes one anxiety, tension, pressure, fear, or fear when it overthinks an anxiety disorder. It is not just too much worrying about something - it is so concerned with something that it affects, impacts or destroys one's ability to function in their life.

When you're wondering or concerned about yourself, your job, your family, your friends, or anything else, and you don't have a pessimist thinking problem, whatever you're thinking about, you're worried for a while, then you're moving on with your day after a short period of time. Sometimes you continue to worry, but you don't ruminate endlessly.

You find the stress doesn't interfere with the rest of your life. Nevertheless, with pessimist thinking because of an anxiety disorder, the concern is all that the person can think about, and although they may not obsess with the same thing all the time, they are always worried about anything. If you are certain that you may suffer from anxiety pessimist thinking, you may have found that you have experienced or suffered one or more of these situations:-Difficulty observing and contributing to a conversation because you go over and over possible answers or comments until the discussion has either ended or the window of opportunity to respond has been missed-Continuously compare yourself Furthermore, all those who do experience it will find that their quality of life is affected by their inability to control negative thoughts and emotions effectively. It can make it harder to go out and socialize, enjoy sports, or be productive at work because their mind spends excessive time and energy on different thought lines. There is a feeling of not having complete control over their own minds or thoughts, that can be very toxic or damaging to one's mental health.

Making friends or holding them can be difficult to overthink because you are struggling to communicate when something is wrong, or you may communicate excessively. Speaking to them can be extremely difficult because you are worried about what to do or do with them because you are overly concerned about how you are going to do it or what is going to happen.

Someone pessimist thinking may even struggle to conduct general conversations or interact in a normal environment. We may even have trouble going to the supermarket or making an appointment.

The reality is that pessimist thinking will affect your life on anything and everything. It can affect the way you communicate with others, it can influence your social life, and it can affect your personal life.

What that means is that it can start wearing away at you and your relationships with the people around you. Pessimist thinking, in your life, can create serious problems. Before you can know how to avoid pessimist thinking, you first must ask yourself, "Why do I overthink? "Sometimes pessimist thinking is an anxiety or depression by-product. If that is the case, anxiety or depression may need to be handled to reduce pessimist thinking. You can find that pessimist thinking just materializes that you need to make a tough decision about life or deal with your uncertainty. When pessimist thinking is not a sign of a deeper emotional problem, shifting thoughts and mindsets can often resolve it.

How to Stop Pessimist thinking, "Stop pessimist thinking things!" Maybe you've heard this many time, and it's not helpful enough. You cannot just turn a key around and avoid pessimist thinking. However, being asked to avoid pessimist thinking always ends up with you thinking more about issues. That is a loop of viciousness. Essentially, trying not to overthink yourself is a long process. You got to train your brain to do that. Below are the few reasons why you may overthink and teach how to stop thinking overthrow.

Your mind will race when you can't sleep, and you may have obsessive thoughts about getting sleepy. Often when insomnia strikes, this pessimist thinking comes and then continues with the next day. You can feel tired and less concentrated on your brain. You might have negative thoughts and obsessive thoughts about not sleeping. For a reason, insomnia is called a vicious cycle. It's tough to stop pessimist thinking about not sleeping when you have it. If you have trouble sleeping, here are a few ways you can reduce that.

Apps to meditate and be conscious. They help you live in the present moment, discarding any intrusive thoughts or feelings you may have.

Apart from the fact that your mindfulness can train your brain, it can also calm you down and make sleeping easier. If you can't fall asleep, get out of bed. If you're in your room to sleep and you can't fall asleep, it sounds like you can't pass out. The subconscious connects the restlessness of your brain. Get out and do relaxing things. Don't spend time or do something distracting on social media. Instead, just relax. Realize that you won't die of sleeplessness. While you are told by your fear and anxiety that you cannot sleep, most cases are temporary. While your health is declining as a result of chronic sleep deprivation, too much worry about an occasional bout of insomnia will make the problem worse. If the issue persists, then it is time to see a doctor or therapist.

Another reason people overthink is that they make decisions. Often, it's a big decision. Sometimes, rather stupid decision-making is over something, like what restaurant to choose. While you ought to think about your decisions, it's time to overthrow them, particularly if you have plenty of people waiting for you to make the decision. Here's how to end up overcoming anxiety in decision making.

Make the decision-making time-limit. Fortunately, it doesn't have to be a very short period that you feel extremely rushed, but it should be quick enough to help you stop worrying. Most people, especially the big decision-makers, plan their thought times and, in the meantime, end up distracting themselves. To have other moments to think will prevent anxiety from overthrowing. Again, it can help to be conscious and live in the present moment. The present moment will contain the reasoning behind the decision-making, not the irrational concerns you might have. In some scenarios depending on the situation, you may be able to change your mind about a decision. To realize this can make decision making easier.

7.2 Anxiety and Frustration

Many mental illnesses can lead to pessimist thinking, and there is an obvious connexon between anxiety and pessimist thinking. Those who are nervous shall never live in the present. Parts of the brain are always worried about what's going on next, and extreme anxiety and pessimist thinking will make it difficult to leave home. Here's how to avoid and overthink fear when your nervous brain tells you no.

• Set small goals. Your anxious mind may overthink things by setting goals too big. Anxiety and pessimist thinking make it difficult for you to set bigger targets. You will work your way up by setting smaller goals.

• Again, the importance of meditation and mindfulness cannot be emphasized. For many mental illnesses, it is helpful, especially when it comes to anxiety and pessimist thinking. Meditation will bring you back from the self-made scenarios in mind to the present moment and, should anxiety hit, relax your body.

• Figure what's causing your brain to overthink. Triggers will make your mental illness worse, making it easier to handle it by spending time writing down what causes your distress and overthrowing it.

• Distractions in anxiety and pessimist thinking are always important. Why you should actually begin to pay attention to your issues, distractions will help to reduce your anxiety, tension, and other problems. Try to watch a video, or work on a puzzle.

• Start knowing when an anxiety attack rumble. Then, just try to get out. Anxiety and pessimist thinking can often be avoided, especially when you know what the causes are.

• If your anxiety and pessimist thinking is too great and takes up your whole time, it's time to see a therapist.

Anxiety, Frustration, and pessimist thinking are two things that go hand in hand, but you can make it much easier by controlling your anxiety and pessimist thinking.

When one thinks about multi polar disorder, they tend to think of the details they have about mental health. And that information regarding wellbeing is the fact that people with multi polar disorder appear to be either depressed or manic. Those with it are having a hard time with their mood, but with pessimist thinking, they may also have a hard time. In multi polar disorder, mind-boggling or distressing thoughts may occur on both sides of the coin. Depression can cause one to worry about what will happen in the future. Or, they may be worried about the side effects of the drug that they are taking. With mania, you may find it difficult to pay attention to your thoughts, making it more difficult to challenge your thoughts. Sometimes it's hard to separate real life from fiction. Or, you may be so euphoric that you spend time to feel safe, and then regret it. If you are affected by multi polar disorder, it is critical that you seek online therapy or an in-person therapist for help. For mild to moderate cases, online therapy works especially well. A therapist can give you basic information about multi polar disorder and mental health information. Plus, it's important that you pay attention to your feelings.

Your depressive symptoms can sometimes last for different periods of time, and your emotions can make them worse. You may focus on the negative and cause long periods of time to worsen your disorder.

Our thoughts that pop into our minds, multi polar disorder or not, tend to make the problem worse. If you need it, then seek help. Positive Thinking Thoughts You may wonder how you can stop pessimist thinking. One way to think is through more positive thoughts.

You could roll your eyes to that. You assume that, by definition, positive thoughts are straight out of a cheesy book on wellness. Science, however, supports that the key to success is positive thoughts and more positive thinking patterns. If you want to change your mind set in positivity, here are a few ways of doing that.

• Look at the prejudice on the confirmation. Negative thoughts tend to linger, and the reverse is generally the case when it comes to positive thoughts. You should try to change the thought around a little bit.

• Continue hearing your positive thoughts instead. Write that down when you start thinking positively. Notice when you think positive thoughts, and compile all of them.

• We can't stress enough on that. Practice patience. Reflective methods allow you to let go of any emotional distress. A disturbing idea passes through the glass. Focus your thoughts on the positive.

• Think about all those times you helped people. Just think of something that will make you happy. Any worrying thoughts just let go. It is a series of measures that require practice.

• Many people believe positive thinking does not mean pessimist thinking at all. Anything that concerns should be ignored, however big it may be. That is not true. Positive thinking simply means having less pessimist thinking within the pessimist thinking department. It's going to happen distressing feelings, but positive thinking tells us that emotional distress is temporary and that there's a lot to think about.

• Try to clean up your Social Media feed. Eliminate the more negative people and concentrate on positivity. Yeah, you can absorb negative news too, but it overloads other people, and if you're an over thinker, it's not good for you.

Mentally Strong People Fortified emotionally are less likely to overthink. Think about how muscular your brain is. The more you train it, the better you are going to get mentally. It's particularly important to increase the strength of your mental health as you age. Mental health declines with aging, but you can train your mind with the right health information. For your mind, here's some good mental health information: • Mentally strong people do a lot of exercises. When you think about exercise, you can imagine that strong people will improve your body. Exercise, however, has a lot of positive side effects for your mind. Your brain, for example, releases good chemicals that kill pain and help lower your hormones of stress. Exercise, not to mention, helps distract you from your emotions, making it great if you want to know how to stop pessimist thinking.

Mentally strong people fully try to socialize possible. Try to talk to a close friend and go further into meeting them. In your social circle, you don't have any friends to talk with, try to get out and talk to someone in a bookstore, cafe, or somewhere else. As you talk to other people and try to make friends, you feel a lot less anxiety and more being in the know. Those with strong mental wellbeing undergo cognitive behavioural therapy daily. A type of therapy helps you get rid of bad habits and feelings and can be used to treat mental illness of all types. Eating disorders, multi polar disorder, generalized trouble with anxiety, and more.

Fortified people tend to train themselves by mixing it up mentally. Over and overdoing the same things will have negative side effects. Look at the positive aspect of your life and think differently about what you can do. Seek a new hobby, go for your dream job, or actually learn something new.

Once you start living for a new day, it helps to overthink yourself. Strong people seem to know that times of vulnerability are about to come. There are moments when you spend too much time worrying, and you then find that you overthink yourself. It will happen, and you can't overthink this. It does happen occasionally. Don't just spend hours at it. You can arrange a period to let your mind wander about a issue, and then stop thinking about it when that time is up. This may take practice, but it can certainly be done by strong people.

Reduce stress You might wonder why there's "reduce stress" on here. Okay, pressures go hand in hand with our propensity to overthink. Stress is the way our body protects us when we're over our heads in a situation that scares us, but our body can't tell the difference between real danger and normal issues, so the stress piles on. People tend to have trouble dealing with all their pressures. Stress can be therapeutic for some. Positive psychology-related stress, which is positive stress, helps to push you and make you want to do better. Yet positive psychology goes only so far.

Too much pessimist thinking, and stress can make your problems worse instead of making them easy, which includes:
• Making you afraid of rejection, shame, disappointment, or losing everything. You tend to worry about unchangeable issues. Most people realize they should be worried about the things they can change and ignore the things they can't change, but that's hard to overthink. Physical stress is an over-stressing epidemic. This hurts every day, literally. Physical stress means stress has intense, actual effects. Physical stress manifestations include headaches and other body aches, which can also be clinical depression. Stress can befall anybody.

Whether you are a child, in your teen years, or an adult, it does not matter. If you're getting used to pessimist thinking and having stress, here are some simple ways to reduce stress. Anyone can do these simple ways, and neither do these simple ways involve a doctor. Cognitive-behavioural therapy. This is something that takes practice, but it's important to learn to identify thoughts that are, by definition, intrusive and to learn how to cope with these thoughts. Write down the issues and order them from the most critical to the least. A part of solving problems involves first solving the easiest issue and moving on. Soon, problem-solving will be easy. Consider your fear of failure and other daily fears. Why are you so afraid? How is it that depression affects you? Were you afraid of remorse, loss, or anything more? People do not understand the importance of working out. By quire a little, it can help to reduce the tension. Take time to relax. See what's going on at your favourite show. Don't waste too much procrastinating time but take a break and come back with a fresh mind instead. Do not take alcohol or drugs. Consider this if talking to a doctor or counsellor causes them to prescribe medication. Try to work with a counsellor at last. Maybe they can support you with your issues.

Hypochondria The hypochondria is another aspect of pessimist thinking and generalized anxiety disorder in general. This is when you still worry that you have something wrong with them medically, which makes it a big problem to overthink.

A few individuals are slightly hypochondriac. For example, you might think something is wrong with you, usually, after you have paid Rd. Google a visit, so you're talking to your doctor. Instead, you'll find that nothing is wrong, and it's just an issue with pessimist thinking, mixed in with a touch of generalized anxiety.

You could be a severe hypochondriac, though. You're still talking over something with your doctor today. You still have those feelings after you talk to your doctor, and there seems to be no discussion with your doctor to make them go away. You still think you are sick, no matter how much you try. That's something you need to get help with. More than a generalized anxiety disorder, you may have. You can finally work up the courage by getting therapy to admit you are fine.

Seek Motivation Although many people are sceptical about motivational speakers; they can help. You can be encouraged to read articles, stories about a man who has managed to overcome fear and endure or people who have learned to start living at an older age and are another good way to distract you from pessimist thinking. It's a good way to get some personal level of mental health knowledge. Although some of this information about mental health may not be a part of contemporary psychology, some are worth checking out. Learn all the knowledge you can get on your health when it comes to mindfulness. Some books are short, and it doesn't take that much time to read. Rest takes a lot of time, but it's worth the information they give. Many self-help books sound a bit cheesy, but you'll be surprised how much healing, rejection, shame, disappointment, and other things can help.

When it comes to pessimist thinking, it's best to absorb all the material you can have in mindfulness. Being alert is the key to getting the help you need. Anything Other? It is worth mentioning that the way we think and the way the brain functions is still a mystery. There are many clinical trials that may tell us more about the mind, both psychological, social, and beyond. Such clinical trials, however, are just health, social, and mental trials.

Pessimist thinking is a trait that can happen at any given time. It can also have the symptom of pessimist thinking for someone who has anxiety or any form of anxiety disorder, too.

The anxiety and worry that you have in your life over different situations and different obstacles can quickly turn into pessimist thinking and wondering what you should do or how you can stop bad things from happening. The fact is, you can't stop all bad things happening and you can't stop any bad decision from happening. What you can do is get assistance. If you have struggled to avoid pessimist thinking, it might be helpful to look for professional treatment. There are many places you can find help, but a simple and private place to start is through an online therapy site that can easily found from mental health centres of your area. On that portal or website, you will find access to licensed counsellors ready to help you overcome your pessimist thinking struggles. You don't need to self-stop your thoughts. Trust an online therapist to lead you towards a healthy way of thinking about your life and a healthier way of living your life every day.

You will be able to communicate with a registered, private mental health provider through online therapy without having to worry about visiting or admitting into a hospital or even being seen by anyone other than the therapist himself. You will feel more comfortable because you are in a place in which you feel best, your home. Not only that, but you will have control over what's happening. All this may make it easier for you to open and start your journey of healing alongside your therapist. So, to overcome all this, you just have to find the right one.

7.3 Identifying Core Objective

How to Discover Your Life Purpose After interacting across the world with more than a million people, I have come to believe that each of us is born with a unique purpose in life. Maybe the most important positive action people take is to identify accept and fulfil this intent.

They take the time to realize what they are here to do –and then, with passion and enthusiasm, they pursue that. Our mission and passion in life are transparent and evident to some of us. We are born with a set of talents, and we develop our talents into skills through persistent exercise. Our children are clear-cut examples of intent. From the moment they were clearly interested in what they got in the world. One child may be wanted to draw all the time, and now he's in the world of art. Another may child has always tapped rhythms on paint cans and dishes, and he and one of his brothers are now in the world of music. May be one child will be in the world of literature, and our other child may be in the world of business. Most of them had natural talents that were clear indicators of what they ended up passionate about. Nevertheless, it's not as easy to identify a passion for some people. At one point, you may even have asked yourself, "What should I do with my life?" What am I enthusiastic about?" Or ' What's my purpose in life.' Instead, you can enjoy what you're doing, although on broader understanding, discover that you're totally different from what you're doing. I'd like to give you tips below to help you find a passion for your life and a true purpose.

7.4 Explore your Favourite Things to Do

We are all born with a profound and deep intent to be revealed. You don't have to make up for your purpose; it's already here.

To create the life, you want, you must uncover it. You may think, "What is my life purpose?" By exploring two things, you will begin to discover your passion or purpose: 1. What do you like doing? What's simple for you? Of course, developing your talents requires work— even the most talented musician still must practice — but it should feel natural, rather than upstream, like rowing downstream.

I love teaching, reading, coaching, facilitating training, and developing lectures, workshops, and classes on transformation. I enjoy bringing together other leaders for conferences and creating new approaches to our work.

To me, these things are easy. While I spent several years learning how to master these skills, I loved it every minute. Work is required, in other words, but suffering is not. When you fail and suffer, you obviously don't live intentionally. What qualities do you enjoy expressing the most in the first world? Ask yourself, what are the two qualities I enjoy expressing in the world? There are peace and happiness. Second, ask yourself, how would I enjoy expressing these qualities in two ways? Mine inspire people and empower them. I inspire people with the compelling story I share in my workshops and write about in my books, and I motivate them by teaching them powerful, successful strategies they can use in their own lives.

Take a few moments to write a depiction of what the world would look like if it worked perfectly, according to you. All are living their highest vision in my perfect world where they are doing, becoming, and doing all they want. Finally, put all three together during one statement, and you'll have a clear idea of your purpose. Mine is "Inspiring and empowering people in a context of love and joy to fulfil their highest dream." Follow Your Internal Guidance (What Do You Say Your Heart?) What if I asked You that what do u have within you your own guidance system that can help you get from when you're in life to where you're heading? It's called the inner GPS. Your inner GPS is close to your car or phone's GPS network. This asks you how to get from A to B.

When you get into your car and go to a destination, what's the first thing you're manually entering your GPS? First, this will find your current location.

This gives you directions to where you're going once it's determined where you're. It just needs to know your start location and your end destination for the system to work. By using an onboard computer that receives signals from several satellites and measures your exact position, the navigation system works out the rest. Then it will plan for you a flawless path. All you must do from that point on is to follow the instructions to get to your destination. To go by clarifying your goal, then secure your destination via goal setting, affirmations, and visualization, and then start acting to drive you in the proper direction. You "pass" the destination you want to get to with every image you see. You express an intention any time you express a preference for something. A window-side table, conference front row seats, first-class tickets, an ocean-view room, or a loving relationship. All these images and feelings give the universe requests. If you stay out of its way — meaning you don't interrupt the process with a stream of negative thoughts, doubts, and fears, your inner GPS will continue to unfold the next steps along the way as you move forward.

In other words, if you clarify and stay focused on your vision (with a vision board or meditation you can do this), the exact steps will keep appearing along the way in the form of internal feedback, generating ideas, and new opportunities. Be Clear About Your Purpose in life. When you're clear about what you want and keep your mind constantly focused on it, the way it is going to show up — sometimes just when you need it, not a moment before. You were born with an inner guide that tells you how much joy you feel when you're on or off track. The content that gives you the greatest joy is aligned with your intent and will get you where you want to go. You'll be surprised and pleased with what it offers as you lose your goals to the world with all its powerful technology. The wonders and miracles are really occurring here.

Take time to think honestly and openly about where you are and what you want to do with your life now. What's the financial status of you? How are the relationships you have? What's your wellbeing like? And so on. Think about where you want to be next. What would it feel like if your life were perfect right now? What kind of career would you have and where are you going to live? You will send powerful trigger points to your subconscious mind by constantly doing this exercise to help you get there.

Conclusion

This book gave you every untapped detail that how you should work on identifying the root cause of the pessimist mindset and the mechanism to work on it. Flow shows that you should first identify the cause then you will be able to identify what category of pessimist mindset you are suffering from and the relevant exercises for the mental health. Once you will opt the suggested Habits Switcher, your personality will be shifted to autopilot mode and you will feel the tremendous positive energy within.

Bad Habits Switcher or negative minds are not easy to convert or transform, there's a lot of rivalry inside, significant positive attitude is expected, loads of energy, devotion and commitment are needed, social, recreational and physical activities need to be part of everyday routine and mental health exercises need to be preceded which won't cost you anything. If the individual is professional businessmen then it often takes longer to transform habits into good ones than you think, because converting Habits Switcher isn't a piece of cake. In contrast, working with the youngsters is easy because their habits are like smooth sludge that can be easily altered and at the same time, they are keen to consume and adapt positivity. Each time you practice, you'll learn how to boost.

It's easy to figure out how to efficiently transform bad habits or unhealthy habits into good habits, but it takes energy, enthusiasm, motivation, time and energy to invest in. If you wish you to become professionally successful and positive person in your daily life you should not only focus on the external factor, surrounding stakeholders or lame excuses but also need to invest in yourself. You should take as much time as is required regularly and bend backward before you begin to adapt as much as possible.

Pessimist mindset has a direct impact on your Habits Switcher and personality. It can affect self-respect and self-esteem of the person. This book gives you meaningful insight of optimistic thinking and allows you to stop impacting your personality and build your own effective way for transformation. This ensures that your Habits Switcher are likely to have a significant benefit and you can start a journey toward successful life with bright future.

Reference

- The Art of Manliness. (2020). How Habits Switcher Can Change Your Life | Art of Manliness. [online] Available at: **https://www.artofmanliness.com/articles/podcast-581-the-Few-habits-that-change-everything/.**
- Inc.com. (2020). Habits Switcher That Lead to Huge Results. [online] Available at: **https://www.inc.com/nicolas-cole/19-Few-habits-that-lead-to-huge-results.html.**
- freeCodeCamp.org. (2020). How to use Habits Switcher to create a consistent study habit. [online] Available at: **https://www.freecodecamp.org/news/how-to-be-more-consistent-when-learning-to-code/.**
- Psychology Today. (2020). Balancing Optimism and Pessimism. [online] Available at: **https://www.psychologytoday.com/us/blog/the-empowerment-diary/201701/balancing-optimism-and-pessimism.**
- The Sleep Advisor. (2020). Benefits of Waking up Early - Our 9 Tips for Making a Morning Routine. [online] Available at: **https://www.sleepadvisor.org/benefits-of-waking-up-early/.**
- Develop Habits Switcher. (2020). Long-Lasting Benefits of Waking Up Early. [online] Available at: **https://www.developFewhabits.com/benefits-waking-up-early/.**
- Medium. (2020). Usual Tips for How to Change Pessimist Mindset. [online] Available at: **https://medium.com/better-humans/11-ninja-tips-on-how-to-wake-up-early-58d63d3972f3.**
- Geon, (2020). [online] Available at: What-are-daily-Few-habits-that-can-change-kids-life.

www.ingramcontent.com/pod-product-compliance
Lightning Source LLC
Chambersburg PA
CBHW070245220526
45465CB00004B/1533